AMERICAN CAPITALISM
Its Promise and Accomplishment

LOUIS M. HACKER

Professor of Economics
Columbia University

AN ANVIL ORIGINAL
under the general editorship of
LOUIS L. SNYDER

D. VAN NOSTRAND COMPANY, INC.

PRINCETON, NEW JERSEY

TORONTO   LONDON

NEW YORK

To
Blanche and Robert Speckman
and
Blenda Larson
in affection

_____

330.573
H118a

PREFACE

THIS book could have been written in one of many ways
—as a theoretical description of capitalist institutions, as
economic analysis, as an historical exposition with the
whole world as its frame of reference. I have chosen to
discuss the promise and accomplishment of capitalism entirely in terms of American experiences. I hope the reader
will agree that there are sound reasons for such a decision,
if the intention of this series is to be fulfilled—to present
significant aspects of the modern world in terms of historical evolution.

I have tried to avoid involvement in complex and fruit-
less debates. Has capitalism always existed—even in classical times under slavery and in medieval times under
feudalism? Does capitalism continue to survive in Britain,
for example, with the spread of nationalization and increasing decision-making by state authorities? Is there capitalism in the newer countries of the Middle and Far East?

If our intention is to examine the capitalist processes
and set up some standards by which these can be compared with communism, for example, a pure case is obviously required. American experiences furnish that: for
American institutions had their origin entirely in a capitalist climate; again, capitalism has the general assent of
the American people. This is their way of life.

I have sought to describe American economic development in capitalist terms. By this I mean, private accumulation leading to investment; decision-making by private
and corporate groups rather than by government; and the
responsibility of government for protecting the monetary
and credit structure. Such an organization of the economic
world—it is the contention of this book—produces and
advances the welfare of the whole population at the same
time that it protects freedom and individual right and
privacy. In short, capitalism means the intertwining of the
economic and political processes by which, and only by
which, democracy can be sustained.

New York　　　　　　　　　　　　LOUIS M. HACKER
Spring, 1957

TABLE OF CONTENTS

Part I

AMERICAN CAPITALISM

— 1 —

THE CAPITALIST CLIMATE
OF AMERICA

Fortunes and Capital. The creation of private fortunes has been a characteristic of most societies throughout the world and human history. Whatever the motives —whether they have been power, prestige, or security— men have accumulated wealth through conquest, looting, human exploitation, and even trade; usury, or money-lending—most frequently for consumption purposes— has also played its part in this process of the maintenance of an unequal distribution of the income a people has produced.

Private fortunes, as such, do not necessarily constitute capital nor have they had a significant economic role in the history of societies until recent times. Frequently they have been kept idle or hoarded and have been expended only as needs manifested themselves. Usually, they have been squandered—on military adventure, the maintenance of luxury courts and similar institutions, the building of monuments, extravagant personal living. True, such outlays have given employment: but they have not added to the social wealth, that is, the productive capacity, of a people.

Such fortunes and their builders have also existed on the margins of societies, again until recent times. Antiquity, because it was based on slavery, had no place in its scheme for the productive processes. The feudal world, the medieval church, and the absolute monarchies of early modern times were concerned with functions and utilized sanctions that also were nonproductive in our modern sense. Consequently the role of the acquisitor was short-lived: he was tolerated, although not necessarily recognized socially. And he was despoiled.

The Capitalist. The acquisitor, as capitalist, does not emerge until perhaps as late as the 17th century. True, there were islands—isolated areas—where the capitalist spirit existed as far back as the 12th century. The independent Italian, Flemish, North and South German cities of the Middle Ages pursued the capitalist round of savings, investment, trade, and production, precisely as we understand these concepts today; but when they were absorbed or overwhelmed by monarchies, the Holy Roman Empire, or the Church, that spirit died.

Capitalism. For capitalism to function, the following requirements were necessary. Private property and the resulting unequal wealth and income had to be protected by law. Accumulation had to be linked with both profits from enterprise and savings as a surplus over personal expenditures. A machinery for the exercise of the credit functions—banks as agencies of deposit and discount, or loans—had to be set up. Society on its part had to accept the commitments that the production of goods and services was its chief concern; that welfare and defense were realizable only by these processes; and that it was the responsibility of government to safeguard the integrity of its own fiscal activities—the establishment of a revenue, the servicing of debt, and the money supply.

Under such a regimen fixed wealth could be accumulated, capital improvements could be developed, productivity advanced, and standards of living could be raised; these could be accomplished only in a world which accepted private fortunes and the profit system as socially and morally defensible.

America as the Capitalist Country. Unlike Europe which, by the 17th century was largely freed of feudalism but where noncapitalist institutions and attitudes continued to survive, America was a land where capitalism was able to establish itself from the beginning. Capitalism was accepted morally, legally, and socially in the British mainland colonies of North America without reservation; in consequence, there was no question about its employment as the only organizing principle for the production of goods and services, the distribution of the social product, and the employment of accumulated funds.

The Rejection of Europe. Why was America the capitalist country par excellence? It was because it rejected those parts of European institutions and ideas that were antipathetic to capitalism and adopted those that strengthened it. The European emigrants who came to America in the 17th, 18th, 19th, and 20th centuries were largely the unwanted humble men and women of the countryside and the smaller communities. They left of their own volition or were deported; they came as free men or bondsmen. They came as the victims of war and famine, religious persecution, ecclesiastical and economic oppression, unequal land systems and guild restrictions, or racial discrimination. And they left behind devices and attitudes that had prevented their upward climb or even survival.

Feudalism was largely terminated in Western Europe by the 17th century, although there were many regions where serfdom remained. But medieval land tenure and organization continued to survive. The cultivators of the land were copyholders—long-term tenants—or they were cottagers—laborers who had rights only to a dwelling; the possession of a freehold, the ownership of land in fee simple, virtually was nonexistent. At the same time, common lands were still open, but increasingly the large landlords were seizing, or "enclosing," them; this meant that cultivators were finding it difficult to pasture their animals and to obtain wood for fuel, construction, and fencing. Nevertheless, the cultivators lived in villages and the villages controlled planting programs.

The Freehold in America. The emigrant could leave all this behind when he came to America. He could become a freeholder, a revolutionary idea, and he did so whether initially as bondsman, squatter, homesteader, or purchaser. This was America's most significant attraction and it was this, largely, that drew the tens of millions of emigrants out of the British Isles, Germany, Scandinavia, and Central Europe for 250 years.

Owning a freehold meant, further, the abandonment of the old manorial and communal practices which had been retarding European agriculture. The result was, the American did not have to settle in a village, observe the village planting program, or pay dues—whether in

work or cash—to the landlord for the use of his public
utilities. He could live where he pleased—and he chose
to live in the center of his farm away from his neighbors; he could plant what he pleased—and more and
more he chose to grow staples as cash crops; he had
water rights, subsoil rights, and the rights to bequeath
and divide his property as he willed. Acquisition was
unencumbered; and a freeholder at the same time was
a freeman.

American Fear of Monopoly. The newcomers also
left behind other economic and social European institutions which were feudal hangovers. Europe was organized in corporations—in industry, trade, the Churches,
and the State; and as feudalism dissolved, the special
privileges that have been associated with these corporations persisted, nevertheless.

Thus the guilds, with their control over wages, ap-
prentices, production, and new capital investments, were
not brought over to the New World. Whether as enterpriser or worker, the American again was a free man:
to set up his own shop, to move about, to trade where
and when and under whatever conditions he pleased.
The European system of monopolies Americans regarded
with suspicion. Corporate charters (in Europe they usually meant exclusive privileges) were granted only with
the utmost caution in early America. Indeed, it was not
until the mid-19th century that legislatures were ready
to enact general enabling laws that permitted corporations to arise, without legislative restrictions, in industry
and commerce. The passage of the Sherman Antitrust
Act in 1890 and its subsequent amendments represented
the prevailing American attitude toward concentration.

The Dignity of Labor in America. The dignity of
labor—and with it the accumulative process—also was
a unique characteristic of the American world. It is true
that the whole Christian system of ethics underscored
the idea; notably Protestantism, because it linked salva-
tion with a "calling" (useful labor), did much to en-
noble man in his humble pursuits. Practices and profes-
sions, however, did not go hand in hand. The medieval
serf was brutalized and exploited. The 17th and 18th centuries saw little improvement in the lot or the status of
labor.

In fact, the theory of mercantilism essentially accepted the debased position of the working classes. Mercantilism—assuming that the wealth of the world was fixed—constantly sought redivisions through foreign trade. A nation's foreign trade could expand—at the expense of its rivals—only as it kept its own costs of production down. The wealth of the nation, therefore, was in its labor supply engaged in the production of goods and services for export; and the size, docility, and poverty of its workers made possible the riches of the whole nation. It was no accident, in consequence, that Britain referred to its workers as "The Poor."

Under this dispensation, the worker was compelled to labor, either as a free or as a forced hand; and he was held in contempt. He was kept badly fed, ill clad, and wretchedly housed, while moralists constantly called attention to his improvidence and want of industry. Not so in America; it was no wonder that Crèvecoeur could say as late as the last quarter of the 18th century: "Formerly they were not numbered in any civil lists of their country, except in these of the poor; here they rank as citizens . . . they receive ample rewards for their labors; these accumulated rewards procure them lands; those lands confer on them the title of freeman, and to that title every benefit is affixed which men can possibly require." (*See Document No. 1.*)

Legal Protection of Property. An attitude is one thing; the creation of sanctions to make possible its realization is another. It is not enough to accept private striving, accumulation, and inequality of rewards based on accomplishment. A legal system that will safeguard these is indispensable to capitalism. This legal system the Americans inherited from Britain; to this extent the mainland colonies were among the leading beneficiaries of the English Revolution of 1688. That revolution once and for all terminated the absolutist monarchy; it ringed around private wealth and income all sorts of protective devices against the predatory assaults of crown, privilege, and star chambers.

The Rule of Law, by curbing arbitrary conduct and by setting up exact procedural guarantees, assures the individual his private rights: of conscience, association, speech, and property. The Rule of Law, through the

creation of constitutional government, imposes limits on
the fiscal powers of public authority. In such a climate
of freedom, rights, and obligations, capitalism thrives.
Such were the favorable circumstances of its establishment and growth in America.

— 2 —

THE COLONIAL ECONOMY

Capital and Labor. Every aspect of capitalist enterprise assisted in the successful establishment of colonial America: capital and labor flowed overseas to
create settlements and these could be made permanent
because of the bountifulness of nature. The capital came
from Britain in large part: in the form of the outlays
of chartered companies and the investments of so-called
proprietors; these made possible the erection of "plantations" in Virginia, Massachusetts, New Amsterdam (New
York) and New Sweden (Delaware) by the first and in
Maryland, Pennsylvania, the Carolinas, and New Jersey
by the second.

Labor came from Britain initially and then increasingly from Germany and Ulster in Ireland. Men and
women set out for America as free men, although, in
the 17th century, the larger proportion were transported
as indentured servants. An indentured servant could not
pay his own transportation; he worked off these costs,
therefore, as a bonded servant. But at the end of the
indenture (running on an average four years) he was a
free man and received "freedom dues"—a small tract
of land, some agricultural implements, clothes. In the
18th century, most of the settlers coming to Pennsylvania were such bondsmen (here they were called "redemptioners") and whether they received land or not,

they settled on it as squatters. Squatters and squatter rights from the beginning affected the history and shaped the legal institutions of America.

Slaves. The flow of indentured servants tapered off not because of a decline in demand for agricultural workers but because a new source of supply appeared—the African Negro slaves. Negro slaves offered many advantages over white servants: they were property and they and their children could be sold and bequeathed; they could not escape easily; their women could also be workers in the fields. With the regularization of supply, in the last quarter of the 17th century, as a result of the activities of chartered companies, a steady flow of slaves overseas could be maintained. Negroes were used primarily as field hands in the tobacco fields of Virginia and Maryland and the rice fields of the Carolinas (and in the sugar cultivation of the British West India possessions); but they were also trained as skilled workers in many crafts. By the middle of the 18th century there were some 500,000 Negro slaves in the mainland colonies.

Natural Resources. The raw materials of America were rich; the application of capital and labor to them began to create the wealth upon which settlement could be founded. The soil, when planted, could sustain life and at the same time produce the staple crops of tobacco, rice, and indigo that could become articles of commerce; there were bog iron deposits everywhere; and America possessed great stands of timber—for wood, shipbuilding, and naval stores—the furs and hides of wild animals and the extraordinary fishing grounds off Newfoundland. The pioneering round of self-sufficiency was quickly replaced by a commercial economy, although cycles of primitive culture—for western lands were constantly being penetrated and brought under the plough—and market economy existed side by side in America up to the end of the 19th century. When the frontier was wholly gone, only then did self-sufficiency disappear as a significant characteristic of settlement.

Trade. The mobility of capital and labor to further economic penetration and production has been alluded to; trade quickly joined them to complete the process. The basic market for American produce was Britain; by

the same token, Britain was the only source of those
finished goods—ironware, textiles, notions, luxury goods
—the young America required. But because the balance
of payments in these exchanges was unfavorable to the
colonies, American trade had to spill over into other
markets. In short, in the triad of capital, labor, and trade,
the last did not have full mobility; and this circumstance
was at the heart of the problem involving the colonies
and the mother country and leading to the First American Revolution.

The following were the significant industries of colonial America linked with trade.

Furs. Colonial America abounded in wild life
which was utilized for furs and hides. The beaver was
the most important fur-bearing animal and it was significant because its pelt was used in hat-making. The
deer, particularly abundant in the south, was hunted
for his hide, used in the making of leather. In the beginning, the pioneering farmers were their own hunters
and trappers; but as farm lands replaced forests and the
tide of settlement pushed inland, the gathering of furs
and hides became a commercial venture. The Indians
became the center of the fur trade, either bringing their
peltries and skins to forts or selling them to agents who
came to their communities. Trade goods, guns, and rum,
in turn, became the substance of the fur trade. The role
of rum is to be noted; it figured in almost all the multilateral trades the American colonists had to develop to
balance their payments with Britain and to make possible
the continued importation of capital.

Lumbering. A new country needs great quantities
of wood (or its substitute): for houses, fences, utensils,
and implements. The ash of hardwoods furnishes potash
and pearl ash for soap-making and textiles. Softwoods
yield tar, resin, and pitch, those naval stores to make
wooden ships sea-worthy. Wood is burned to create
charcoal and so to make iron. For containers, wood
supplies barrels, staves, hoops, and heads. At first as
an adjunct to farming, quickly as an independent business enterprise, lumbering appeared and many of its
products and by-products entered into commerce. To
Britain went the naval stores and the potash and pearl

ash; into the West India trade entered the barrels, staves, and the like.

Lumbering also made possible the appearance of a great shipbuilding industry, and the yards of New England, New York, and Philadelphia became justly famous. American ships made possible the fishing industry of New England. Equally important was the export of ships to Britain, for with the virtual disappearance of the British woodlands, the mother country was hard pressed to take care of her own needs. American ships more and more became the carriers of the trade between metropolis and colonies; at least 30 per cent of the whole English merchant marine had been constructed in American yards during the colonial period.

Fishing and Whaling. In the teeming off-shore waters of New England and in the Great Banks off Newfoundland were to be found mackerel, bass, herring, halibut, sturgeon, and, above all, the mighty cod. New England fishermen fished to eat and fished to sell; and a large and well-capitalized industry sprang up in consequence. Supplies (including rum) had to be sent to the vessels fishing the Banks; back came packed and salted fish to be sold to the Catholic countries of Europe and the slave plantations of the West Indies. The New England exports of fish soon exceeded those of the mother country. Just before the Revolution, there were 665 vessels in the New England fishing fleets and another 350 ships carried fish into foreign commerce.

Whaling soon attracted the New England sailors: for whales furnished oil (illuminants and lubricants) and fins (for buttons and stay-supports). Whales were hunted all over the Atlantic, and some 360 vessels were engaged in the industry. At least 4,000 tons of whale oil went to England annually.

Iron. It was not difficult for the colonies to engage in iron production because of the rich supplies of bog iron and limestone beds and wood. The charcoal made from the last, mixed with the iron and limestone, made excellent pigs, which were produced in country furnaces. Out of the pigs at these furnaces were made hollow ware (pots, pans, stove plates, and firebacks); at forges, the pigs were hammered into bars and sold to blacksmiths to be beaten into farm implements. The industry was situated in the country because of its dependence upon charcoal: therefore a large number of small furnaces and forges existed throughout the colonies. We are talking of heavy iron entirely; the hardware of commerce—the finer tools and instruments, as well as wire and pins—was not made at home but bought as the most important import from the mother country.

Large amounts of capital were attracted to the iron industry. It was not uncommon for merchants, notably in Pennsylvania, to invest in these so-called iron plantations on which were located the workers who frequently were paid in goods from the plantation stores. The American iron industry attracted English attention early, for both the ironmasters, the makers of heavy iron (who looked askance on American competition), and the ironmongers, the makers of hardware (who wanted cheaper pigs and bars), were concerned. In 1750 a policy was finally formulated in the so-called Iron Act which favored the ironmongers: colonial pigs were put on the English free list and Americans were forbidden to erect slitting and rolling mills, plating forges, and steel furnaces. This was an example of the encouragement of the production in the colonies of raw or semi-finished materials and the restraints put on the manufactures in them of finished goods that was at the heart of British policy; and this was precisely the reason why the colonial-imperial relations could not be maintained.

Rum Manufacture. Reference has already been made to the fact that the colonials had to engage in multilateral trades. One of the most important, as we shall see, was with the foreign colonies in the West Indies. From these they brought back molasses and the molasses was distilled into rum. Such distilleries notably sprang up in New England; by 1750 Massachusetts possessed some 60 and Rhode Island some 30. The manufacture of rum soon became the most important single industrial activity of New England. Rum was at the basis of the trades with Indians, the Newfoundland fishermen, and the African slave traders.

Colonial Agriculture. In a capitalist economy, agriculture even in a pioneering setting, cannot remain for long, on a self-sufficiency basis. Even if the farm-stead is obtained free, cash still is required: for taxes, iron, livestock, medicines, and the like. And if clothing and house furnishings are to be acquired, this only strengthens the need for producing cash crops. In consequence, all over colonial America, farm surpluses were being gathered together for shipment to urban communities and for entry into foreign trade. A merchant class thus sprang up—to buy farm commodities, render them into articles of commerce (grain, for example, has to be ground, flour bolted, bread baked), supply the countryside with its needs, and advance credit. A merchant, at the same time, could be and was a dealer in farm commodities, a miller and bolter, a retail-store operator, a wholesaler, a banker, and an importer and exporter. Specialization in all these functions did not appear until much later in America.

Colonial agriculture, in consequence, produced surpluses. New England and the Middle Colonies grew the products of general farming. In the Southern Colonies the plantation wares of tobacco, rice, and indigo were grown. The Northern agricultural goods consisted of beef cattle, hogs, and work animals (horses and oxen); country produce—cheeses, dried fruits, flaxseed, honey; and wheat. Beef and pork products were salted and packed and sent overseas to Newfoundland and West India; work animals were also exported to West India; and flour became a significant article of foreign commerce as well. In the case of flour, because of superior soil and the existence of a large agricultural labor supply (the redemptioners), the colonies of New York and Pennsylvania were particularly important.

Plantation Economy. The great cash crops of colonial America, however, were tobacco first and rice second. These were produced on plantations, which, of course, were organized on a capitalist basis with the capital fund invested not in land or machinery but in slaves. If we see the slaves as capital, then we strike at once at the heart and dilemma of the slavery institution. In a new country like America land costs were cheap and the need for maintaining the productivity of the soil—by drainage, fertilizers, crop rotation—was not pressing. Once the soil was depleted, the plantation could move on.

But if slave costs mounted—the planter's real capital investment—such a fixed charge was a growing burden on the whole economy. There were hidden costs also associated with slavery: the care and maintenance of the young, sick, and superannuated slaves; the conspicuous consumption (in order to assure status) of the slave owner; and the high price of credit—to finance slave purchases, the sale of the crop, and the buying of plantation necessities and home luxuries. Because of all these elements of costs, the plantations were forced to produce only the cash crops. When cotton replaced tobacco in the South, corn was also grown; but only as an animal feed for the work animals used in the fields.

Even as early as colonial America, the plantation owner was under these pressures: some, therefore, engaged in western land speculation to obtain additional income and capital; some ultimately abandoned tobacco —as did Washington; and some continued to grow tobacco and went bankrupt—as did Jefferson. Tobacco notably flourished in Virginia and Maryland, and its export to England constituted the largest single commodity entering in this bilateral trade. On the eve of the Revolution the two colonies were sending to England about 85 million pounds of tobacco leaf; these were processed in England to be sold at home and for re-export. Rice was somewhat similarly circumstanced. It was grown on large plantations in the Carolinas (indigo also was cultivated); but rice was shipped directly to Europe and the Azores.

Basic Role of Credit.   Reference has been made to credit; the plantation system found it to be its life blood. English merchants not only furnished the credit but acted as the commission merchants handling the crop; in fact, they were bankers, commission men, insurance brokers, shippers, and supply houses all rolled into one. Credit and debt are two sides of the same coin; and with the ordinary use of credit, debt mounted. On the eve of the Revolution, of the some £5,000,000 owed by Americans to English merchants, five-sixths of this amount was to be found in the Southern colonies.

Planters, in consequence, had many grievances: the high price of credit, the low prices they received for their crops (they accused English merchants of conspiring to fix prices), the inadequate money supply, market restrictions. There were many reasons why colonials combined to throw off the restraints of the imperial system and to free themselves of the British crown; and these economic pressures played their part.

— 3 —

THE FIRST AMERICAN REVOLUTION

Colonies under Mercantilism. Had capitalism, in the 17th and 18th centuries, been functioning in an international community where capital, trade, and labor moved freely, undoubtedly there would have been no American Revolution. Not that the three thousand miles of separation between mother country and colonies had not produced other areas of disagreement; those that affected politics, however, could have been settled amicably. For both were committed to the ideas of English constitutionalism.

The governance of the economic relations of the empire—in terms of that policy earlier referred to as mercantilism—inevitably created a sense of dependence and frustration on the part of colonial merchants and planters and one of superiority on the part of the metropolis. If, under mercantilist doctrine and policy, the wealth of a nation was represented by a favorable balance of trade, then the part played by the plantations overseas was fixed. Colonies were to produce (and to be encouraged by bounties to do so) raw materials, notably those the mother country traditionally had been acquiring abroad; colonies were to buy—but not manufacture for themselves or acquire from foreign countries—the finished ware the mother country's industry was capable of producing; colonies were not to live beyond their means,

but were to pay their balances to the metropolis in sterling
and, if they needed credit—instead of their own banking
institutions or the monetization of public debt—they were
to resort only to the mother country. Colonies, in short,
existed for the enrichment of the economy at home just
as also did the docile (and low-cost) labor supply. (*See
Document No. 2.*)

The Navigation System.   To accomplish these ends,
the so-called Navigation System was devised. It was made
up of a complex system of statutes—the first passed in
1651 with additions being made throughout the next
one hundred years—which put the management of
colonial economic affairs under the Lords Commissioners
of Trade and Plantations in London.

This system controlled trade and the ships moving in
it. Only English vessels could engage in trade with the
oversea dominions or bring back colonial products into
the mother country; the same restrictions applied to the
produce of Asia, Africa, and all the Americas. As for
European commodities, only certain ones were admitted
to England, and if they were destined for the colonies
they had to be transhipped by way of the mother country.

The system also controlled colonial production. Written
into the acts were so-called "enumerated lists" which
included raw materials grown or created in the colonies;
these could be exported to England alone. In this way,
England—in proper mercantilist fashion—hoped to free
herself of dependence upon the naval stores, spices, min-
erals, and timber of other lands; and the carriage of these
wares earned shipping charges for English vessels. Beginning with 1660 and continuing up to 1764, the following products of colonial origin were put on and added
to these "enumerated lists": sugar, cotton, tobacco, gin-
ger, indigo, dyewoods, rice, molasses, naval stores,
hemp, masts and yards, copper ore, beaver and other
furs, whale fins, hides, lumber, raw silks, potash and
pearl ashes. In short, virtually all the surplus products
of the American colonies—except flour, meat stuffs, and
fish—in time fell under the controls of the Navigation
System.

Bounties.   To keep the colonies tied to raw-material
production, bounties were offered in some instances and
protection against competition in others. As early as

1705, bounties were being given for the raising and making of hemp, tar, pitch, and resin. Attempts were made to encourage the development of wine and silk—with, however, no results. In the case of tobacco, its growth was banned in Great Britain and Ireland in order to give the colonies a clear field. But tobacco was an "enumerated" commodity and, in consequence, could be shipped only to Britain with the real profits from its cultivation accruing therefore to the mother country.

Manufacturing.   The restriction of colonial enterprise to noncompetitive fields or to those which could supplement the economy of Britain thus is revealed. Through the agency of the Lords Commissioners of Trade and Plantations a careful watch was kept on colonial assemblies lest they take actions inimical to the home interests. The Commissioners reviewed colonial legislation to recommend approval or disapproval by the Privy Council; they drew up instructions for the colonial governor; they passed on petitions of English companies seeking to invest in new enterprises in America. (*See Document No. 3.*)

Again and again the colonies—imitating the mother country's example—sought to encourage manufactures by the characteristic mercantilist devices of bounties, premiums, and monopolies; against these the Commissioners moved regularly. At their request the Privy Council "disallowed" a Pennsylvania law to encourage shoemaking, a New York law to encourage sail cloth manufacture, a Massachusetts law to encourage linen production. In 1756, the Commissioners said plainly: "The passing of laws in the plantations for encouraging manufactures, which any way interferes with the manufacture of this Kingdom, has always been thought improper, and has ever been discouraged."

Parliament, in general cases, was resorted to. In 1699 the Woolen Act forbade the movement of colonial wool, woolen yarn, and woolen cloth in intercolonial or international trade. In 1732 the Hat Act similarly banned the shipment of hats and reduced their manufacture to local and custom-made proportions. The Iron Act of 1750, as we have seen, had it that colonial ironmasters could not expand their operations or enter into the fields of wrought ironware and finished steel.

The Balance of Payments. We have been talking
here of trade largely, and that is proper; for the economy
of the 17th and 18th centuries was a commercial one.
Businessmen were called "merchants" and they were
chiefly traders rather than fabricators; the outstanding fortunes of the period were mercantile in origin.
Businessmen, to continue to function, particularly in a
climate of restraint and regulation like the mercantilist
system, had to open up new channels of trade constantly
in order to make profits and to adjust their economy's
balance of payments. For the colonial balance of payments with the mother country was unfavorable: the
colonies bought more goods and services from the
mother country than they sold to it.

At first blush, this would seem not to have been the
case of the Southern Colonies: they exported directly
large quantities of tobacco, rice, naval stores, indigo,
furs, and hides. But almost all their invisible services—
shipping, brokerage, commissions, credit—were acquired
from Britain. We have two clues to the fact that the
Southern Colonies also were in an unfavorable balance:
their constant money stringency (indicating that sterling
flowed overseas) and the piling up of their short-term
and long-term debts to Britain.

As for the Northern Colonies, few of their products
were wanted by England; on the other hand, they had
to acquire their hardware, textiles, house furnishings, and
the like there. The Northern merchant had to develop
many multilateral trades to obtain the specie and bills
of exchange with which to discharge his obligations in
Britain. As long as he could freely do so, the colonial
economy could expand, accumulation could take place,
and capital investments and new enterprises could be
launched. Up to 1763—the end of the Seven Years' War
—no real restraints existed, and the relations between
colonies and metropolis were harmonious. After 1763,
they worsened because new fiscal policies coupled with
new restraints narrowed the spheres of operation of
colonial business.

Multilateral Trades. These were the various trades
Northern businessmen developed. From *Newfoundland*
fish was bought; to Newfoundland went provisions, rum,
lumber, fishing tackle, and salt. From the *Wine Islands*

(Azores, Madeira, Canaries) came light and fortified wines and fruits; to them went fish, provisions, live animals, and wood products. From the *South European* countries came lemons, limes, raisins, salt, and olive oil; to them went fish, timber, and rice. In every instance, the balance of payments was in favor of the American merchants and they acquired specie and bills of exchange on London.

Greatest of all of these trades was the triangular one: *colonies–West India–Africa.* On the Guinea Coast of Africa the colonial slave ships picked up ivory, gums, and beeswax and cargoes of Negro slaves which they carried in that famous Middle Passage to the sugar islands of the Carribean. Here they received specie and bills of exchange; here they loaded their decks with the sugar and molasses the Northern distilleries converted into rum. Return voyages brought to the sugar islands all those surpluses of the North which England was incapable of using: lumber, staves, barrel heads and hoops, flour, salted provisions, fish, and work animals.

The significant fact was, more and more during the 18th century, that this triangular trade was being carried on with the foreign sugar islands belonging to Spain, France, Denmark, and Holland. Technically, these islands were closed to colonial trade; but much of seafaring and commerce was illegal during this era when businessmen were merchants. Trade with the enemy during war, smuggling, and even piracy were frequently the activities of men who at the same time had no moral qualms about participating in the unsavory traffic of carrying Negro slaves.

In 1733, Britain sought to check the flow of sugar and molasses from the foreign islands by placing virtually prohibitive duties on the commodities originating there. These laws were not enforced—in large part because, after 1740, England was at war and her navy could not be used as a patrol; in large part because colonials were not averse to smuggling. In effect, therefore, this foreign-island commerce sustained colonial prosperity and made possible the payment of balances to England. When after 1763—with peace returning—Britain struck at this business, the whole economic structure of colonial America was shaken.

Control over Currency. An economy with no independent credit machinery of its own and with an unfavorable balance of trade—a debtor nation, in other words—constantly concerns itself with its monetary shortages and seeks escape through the route of inflation. Tinkering with the currency has been a characteristic of American development from early times and it was not until the 1930s that the demand for more money—as a political issue—receded from the front rank. With no metallic mining resources available to America until the 1850s, and with the dearth of coin common to the whole late 17th and 18th centuries world, colonials resorted to all sorts of devices to expand their currency. It was part of British mercantilist policy to prevent this; and here we have another important center of controversy.

To mercantilism, a favorable balance of payments was represented by settlements in bullion; the mounting gold and silver stocks of a nation exemplified its wealth and the colonies were expected also to operate in these terms. They paid their balances (and later, the taxes imposed after 1763) in specie; nor was specie to be sent out of England to the colonies. In order to keep the colonial money supply tied to the pound sterling, certain other restraining measures were taken.

The colonies could not mint their own coins (in effect, re-mint, for this would have permitted debasement by a lowering of the silver content). Colonies could not revalue (or overvalue) foreign coins; and when they tried to do this in the case of the Spanish milled silver dollar (the piece-of-eight), the crown intervened in 1704 and fixed a uniform table of values for all foreign coins.

The colonies then resorted to paper issues, through so-called bills of credit. These were comparable to our Treasury notes of today—short-term obligations issued in anticipation of tax receipts. Massachusetts was the first colony to do so in 1690; before long all the colonies were following suit. If such bills have fixed terms when they are to be called and if they are not legal tender (to be used in settlement of private debts), they do not add to the money supply. But if the reverse happens—old bills are replaced by new issues; no taxes are earmarked for their retirement; they are accepted in commercial transactions as legal tender—then they become part of the circulating medium. And as they increase, inflation results. (*See Document No. 4.*)

After 1710, this is exactly what happened and the pound sterling began to mount in value as the paper bills depreciated everywhere (except in New York and Pennsylvania). By 1750, a runaway inflation was threatening and the English government formally stepped in. Parliament passed the Currency Act of 1751 which was directed against the New England colonies: they were not to authorize the bills to be used as legal tender; outstanding bills were to be retired at their maturities; and new bills could be issued only when taxes for their retirement were set up. In 1764, the act was made applicable to all the colonies and all bills of credit outstanding were to be retired when due. An enormous shrinkage of the money supply naturally occurred—and this particularly in a period of business recession, for business had contracted (as it usually does after a war) when the Seven Years' War ended. Hard times, little money and little credit, and new taxes—this was part of the background of events that ushered in the fateful twelve years 1764-1776.

Banking. Another device developed in the colonies as an agency of issue was the land bank, which many colonies authorized. Such banks made loans against farm mortgages, issuing notes, and these, too, became legal tender. Massachusetts sought to go further when it chartered a "Land and Manufactures Bank" in 1740: loans, in short, were to be made against both land and nonperishable agricultural commodities. This looked too much like public banking to the mother country; and in 1741—applying the Bubble Act of 1720—England ended the Massachusetts bank. It is important to observe that the young and growing country of America had no public or commercial banks—as a result of English restraint— until the Revolution was virtually over.

Burdens of Empire. After more than a generation of war, Britain emerged victorious, defeating France and Spain and enormously increasing her empire in the east (India) and the west (Canada and the territory to the Mississippi, excluding Florida). She now dominated the world commercially; but she was left with a staggering burden of debt, the need for devising a management for the new territories, and the putting of her own economic house in order as far as the colonies were concerned. British policy during 1763-75 concerned itself with all these problems, and they were in a real sense all aspects of the single one of strengthening her mercantilist system.

For the first time taxes were levied, in 1764 and 1765, the latter including the stamp tax. This was replaced by the so-called Townshend duties of 1767 and the Tea Act of 1773. The colonies were up in arms against these devices because of the failure of consultation ("No Taxation Without Representation"), because the taxes were to be paid in specie—in a time of currency stringency, because they were being imposed in a period of business decline, and because the Tea Act strengthened the hand of the monopoly East India Company in the colonial retail and wholesale trades.

The Government of the West.   To govern the vast new territory that Britain had acquired west of the Appalachians, the so-called Proclamation Line of 1763 that closed this region to new settlements (and to the colonial fur trade) was imposed. Under the Quebec Act of 1774, these lands were put under the administration of Quebec, in Canada; colonials seeking the chartering of land companies to open the territory of the Ohio particularly were given short shrift; and fur traders had to obtain licenses from the same distant authority. Britain argued that such measures were necessary for the ordering of Indian relations; to the colonials they were subterfuges designed to favor British capital and to shut American capital out of this profitable area of expansion.

The West India Trade.   Britain had been troubled by the great increase in colonial trade with the foreign sugar islands, as we have seen. Against this—for it was regarded as illegal—her officialdom moved with energy. Naval patrols were strengthened to stop smuggling; new courts were established (without juries) to try offenders; the customs machinery in the colonies was tightened up; general search warrants ("writs of assistance") were authorized.

The Sugar Act of 1764 strengthened the earlier measure of 1733 by imposing duties on foreign molasses and refined sugar and by forbidding entirely the impor-

tation of foreign rum. In the same act, high duties were
placed on wines from the Wine Islands, on wines, fruits,
and oil imported from Spain and Portugal, and on luxury
goods from France.

Tightening the System. Along with these measures, as has been noted, went the Currency Act of 1764,
and the expansion of the "enumerated list" in 1764 and
1766. The colonies were in the midst of recession: there
were serious business downturns in 1764-69 and in 1772-
75. It was no wonder that businessmen should take
alarm. The protests against the Tea Act of 1773 were
widespread and when Britain retaliated with the so-called
Coercive Acts of the next year, the colonies, meeting
in the First Continental Congress of that year, replied
with an embargo on English goods. The drift into war
thus was taking place; and actual hostilities broke out in
1775. (*See Document No. 5.*)

— 4 —

FOUNDING THE REPUBLIC

Organizing for War. It is not easy for any government to wage war; to carry on a revolution presents
almost insuperable problems. The creation of an army
and its supply; the establishment of a working fiscal program; the conduct of foreign negotiations; the control
of dissent at home at the same time that basic changes
are carried out—for civil war and revolution are two
different things—these are matters requiring the greatest
energy, courage, and devotion.

The American people entered the Revolution as thir-
teen sovereign states bound together in a loose alliance:
the central government, the Continental Congress, was
only the "superintending power." Financing was to be

simplicity itself: the war was to be supported not by taxes
but by requisitions upon the states. It was not until the
Articles of Confederation were ratified, in 1781, that
the Confederation Congress was invested with somewhat
greater authority. The point is, however, that Continental
Congress and Confederation Congress were beset by
mounting difficulties, and, while the war was won in the
field by 1781, the Revolution was in danger of founder-
ing by 1786.

Opponents of the Revolution—the so-called loyalists—
were to be found in all the states, and they were put down
with vigor and harshness. They were arrested, frequently
tried summarily, imprisoned; their property was con-
fiscated and great numbers were driven into flight. Seizure
of property had two purposes: it made possible a redistribution of lands and it furnished funds for the states. It
has been estimated that loyalist property losses ran to
$50,000,000.

Financing the War.   The inability or the refusal of
the states to support the central government and the
army compelled the Congresses to use the familiar devices
of paper issues. Loan certificates, certificates of indebtedness, and bills of credit were emitted; and because there
was no specie backing or regular revenue sources to support them these at once depreciated. During 1775-83,
the Congresses raised something like $82 millions, specie
value, to finance the war. State requisitions brought in
$5.8 millions; domestic loans, $27.3 millions; bills of
credit, $37.8 millions. The bills of credit soon began to
lose value. By 1779, Congress had issued in this paper
$241.5 millions, and the bills were worth then three cents
on the dollar. On March 17, 1780, when the ratio of
paper stood at almost 100 to 1, Congress repudiated
these issues and ordered redemption—through new bills
—at one fortieth of their nominal value.

The states did no better. Their total of paper bills came
to $250 millions and the states, too, took to repudiation.
Virginia (responsible for one-half of the paper) ex-
changed ultimately at the ratio of 100 to 1; the North
Carolina rate was 800 to 1; other states paid off at ratios
varying from 40 to 1 to 100 to 1. By 1782, the state
"old tenor" bills were out of circulation.

Foreign Help.   Fortunately, credit—and therefore

funds for obtaining military supplies—was available abroad. The French crown and private subscriptions turned up $2 millions; the French government—after the treaties of amity and alliance of 1778—lent another $6 millions; the Spanish government lent $200,000. Dutch bankers, after 1781 when the war in the field already was over, produced $1.3 millions. This help—coupled with French military and naval assistance—really turned the tide.

Results of the Revolution. With the defeat of the British in 1781 and the writing of the Peace of Paris in 1783, the war and the Revolution were over. The victories—in addition, of course, to independence—appeared immense. As a result of freedom and the severing of the tie with British mercantilism, the American businessmen had a larger world in which to function. In *foreign trade,* Europe and the East were opened up to American commerce. It was not until the Jay Treaty was completed in 1795, however, that reciprocity was granted in the British trade. In *manufacturing* and *banking,* all restraints were removed, and, although advances were slow in manufactures, there was impressive accomplishment in banking. The states began to charter banks, as did the Congress, first in the Bank of North America and then later in the Bank of the United States. In *agriculture* and the *land,* the seizure of the ungranted crown lands and those of the proprietaries plus the opening up of the trans-Appalachian territory to easy settlement helped fill eastern America with large numbers of farmers. Land reform in the states also terminated the rights of entail and primogeniture. All these created fresh opportunities for capital enterprise and the states helped the process by chartering companies for banking, land development, and public works.

Inadequacies of the Confederation. There was an initial spurt of prosperity with the end of the war; but by 1785, the American economy began to falter. It was clear that the weaknesses of the central government—notably its inability to lay out a sound program of fiscal policy—inevitably undermined confidence. With no powers to tax or in fact to control foreign commerce, no revenues were coming in and no real settlement with Britain was possible.

The Peace of Paris had promised that the pre-Revolutionary mercantile debts would be paid back to British merchants and that the molestation of loyalists (with settlement of their claims legally) would end. Britain held the western posts pending the completion of such agreements; they were not made and, in consequence, the western lands were in turmoil. The inability of the central government to refund the war debts destroyed confidence in it as far as new loan operations were concerned. Nor would foreign private capital risk the opening of new ventures in America. While this was going on, American merchants were piling up huge unfavorable balances abroad. It was becoming evident to the discerning—and Alexander Hamilton understood this—that despite all the new ventures in trade and industry and the great future promise of America, the country was living beyond its means. In 1785 and 1786, specie began to flow out of the country, credit became tight, agricultural prices fell—and the boom was over. (*See Document No. 6.*)

The States' Actions. Almost all the states showed no concern over the incapacities of the Confederation government. Rather than giving it power to control foreign commerce and to impose duties, they did so themselves. There developed a tangle of regulations, imposts, and tariffs; as a result, America had no bargaining power in its effort to obtain most-favored-nation treatment from foreign countries. The states sought to attract foreign commerce away from one another; they quarreled over boundaries and land claims; they could not agree on the regulation of interior waterways.

Then, with recession, the states began to utilize the earlier and disastrous practices of paper emissions and contract violations. By the end of the war, most states had voided their old bills of credit as legal tender. But the outflow of the country's specie and distress in the countryside prompted seven of them to begin the printing of paper once more during 1785-86. A good deal of this paper began to depreciate at once; and the paper of New Jersey, Georgia, and Rhode Island soon became worthless. Rhode Island went so far as to try to compel the acceptance of its bills of credit as legal tender; and the courts were filled with debtors and creditors wrangling with each other.

With paper issues went the demand for stay or mortgage-moratorium laws, and for laws to write down debts and to abolish imprisonment for debt. Mobs and armed troops—as in the rebellion led by Daniel Shays in Massachusetts—marched on courts and threatened to bring the pressures of mob violence on legislatures.

Summoning the Constitutional Convention. It was this state of affairs, plus the breakdown of the central government, that prompted responsible men to seek a strengthening of authority. Currency tinkering and stay laws—paper issues that depreciated and contracts that were violated—jeopardized any chance of economic betterment in America. When the Constitutional Convention met in Philadelphia in 1787, the country already was in crisis and the Revolution—which had established independence and offered a climate of freedom for enterprise—was in danger.

The Constitutional Convention. To save the Revolution against the leveling tendencies in the states, the Constitutional Convention proceeded to establish a central government with energy. The protection of property and the guaranteeing of the fiscal integrity of government were two of its leading concerns and it accomplished these by forbidding the states to issue legal-tender bills of credit and by denying them the right to impair the obligation of contracts. As a result of the latter, only the national government could enact bankruptcy laws and only the federal courts could pass on moratorium laws.

Similarly, the new national government was given positive powers: it could levy and collect taxes; it could place duties on foreign imports; it could regulate interstate and foreign commerce; it could borrow and coin money; it could issue patents and copyrights; it could raise and support armies, manage and sell the public lands, and protect the states from domestic violence. Further, it was given the right to fund the debts contracted by the central government and the states during the revolutionary period.

It is idle to maintain—and this position has been taken —that the Constitution represented the seizure of power by a small, propertied class made up of wealthy merchants, land speculators, and holders of the public debt. This was a *coup d'état;* this was a challenging of the democratic forces in America. The fact is, although the Founding Fathers were conservative, they were also conserving. Unless property were secure and the actions of government in its fiscal relations responsible, the American states could not have endured. There was "a critical period" facing America and only an energetic and honorable government could save the day. This the Founding Fathers understood and this was their great accomplishment; that the government they devised was able to weather all kinds of awe-inspiring difficulties throughout the years is a tribute to their genius.

The Hamiltonian Program.   Alexander Hamilton, George Washington's first Secretary of the Treasury, was the great man who guided the young Republic through its difficult first ten years. He was in office from 1789 to 1795; but his leadership of the Federalist party, for the balance of the decade, made it possible for him to continue to guide policy. These were years of trial, indeed. Relations with England and Spain were still at sixes and sevens; French revolutionary ideas were sweeping the western world, and before long Europe was embroiled in a war that sought to involve America; leveling ideas still were general in the states and threatened the life of the Republic. More particularly, Hamilton's ideas for finance and foreign relations were being regarded with suspicion by a growing group of anti-Federalists, headed by Jefferson and Madison, who soon became the party of opposition known as the Republican party (progenitors of the present-day Democratic party.)

To Hamilton, the new nation could endure only if its conduct was honorable: if it had fiscal integrity and observed a strict neutrality as regards European involvements. A government with energy could do all this: fund its debt, provide revenues for the needs of administration, protect the money supply, regulate foreign trade (which also meant a settlement with Britain), and safeguard its rights. In such a climate, private enterprise could function—for the public credit and private credit went hand in hand—new opportunities for investment could be sought out and foreign capital would enter the United States. Hamilton was no authoritarian and no mercantilist, but a libertarian in the best Adam Smith sense: "a regime of perfect liberty" was the one under which America could maintain its security and advance to prosperity.

Finance. Congress took the first step in passing the Tariff Act of 1789, a measure to which the Confederation Congress could never obtain the consent of the sovereign states. This was devised to raise a revenue and safeguard the American merchant marine; in fact, income from duties continued to be the chief reliance of the federal government. The general run of duties was 5 per cent; a drawback of 10 per cent was allowed on all taxable articles coming in American ships; and a tonnage tax of 50 cents a ton was put on foreign vessels entering American ports. To this income, Hamilton added the system of internal revenues; at his request, Congress placed taxes on whiskey and rum, collectable at the source; and later added taxes on carriages, sugar, snuff, and auction sales. The excise met with strong opposition, and the Whiskey Rebellion of 1794 challenged federal authority. But Hamilton met this uprising quickly and his success assured the general acceptance of the government's right to tax.

No government can endure—this was Hamilton's position in his famous "Report on the Public Credit" of January, 1790—unless it pays regularly its obligations. To assure continued credit, it was necessary that old debt be refunded and even the revolutionary debts of the states be assumed. Such old debt, too, was to be paid off at 100 cents on the dollar and to current holders. True, much of it had been incurred in a depreciated paper and many of the original holders had parted with certificates at fractions of their face value and to speculators. No matter; funding had to take place to protect the honor of the nation.

The problem was gargantuan. Foreigners held $11,700,000 of this paper; $40,400,000 in securities were held by Americans; the outstanding revolutionary debts of the states came to another $25,000,000. On the question of the assumption of the state debts a bitter fight was waged, and Hamilton gained the day only by yielding on another issue—the location of the capital of the new government. The anti-Federalists wanted the capital on the Potomac, obtained this, and acceded on assumption.

Hamilton drove a good bargain with the bondholders: four-ninths of the bonds were to carry 6 per cent interest; two-ninths were to be interest-free for 10 years when 6 per cent was to be paid; and three-ninths were to carry 3 per cent. Of equal importance were provisions for a sinking fund and for open-market operations by the Treasury to protect the bonds' prices. The customs revenues were to be earmarked for interest payments; from the sales of public lands was to be built up the fund for redemption of the bonds.

The Bank. In December, 1790, Hamilton sent his "Report on the Bank" to Congress. He asked Congress to charter a bank with the rights of deposit, discount, and note issue; in effect, such an institution would be a central bank, for it could control the money supply (or credit) of the nation by demanding specie payments on their notes from the state banks. Hamilton saw other purposes for such an agency: it would augment "the active or productive capital of the country"; it could lend to the federal government and facilitate its collections; it would be a government depository.

The anti-Federalists raised the cry of monopoly (although the states were already chartering banks; Pennsylvania, New York, and Massachusetts had done so); but Washington followed Hamilton rather than Jefferson and signed the Bank bill, incorporating it for 20 years. (*See Document No. 7.*)

Under private auspices, the Bank was to have the semi-public functions alluded to. The government could be—and became—a subscriber; foreigners could buy its shares—and did—but they could not become directors. Private persons could pay for their shares in government bonds up to three-fourths of their subscriptions; the rest was to be in specie. The Bank was to be capitalized at $10 millions; could erect branches; and was to engage in the regular banking business of taking deposits, making loans, deal in acceptances and foreign exchange, and the like. It performed all its functions admirably, both adding to the country's currency and regulating the notes of the state banks; by 1796, federal loans by it stood at $6 millions.

Coinage. In January, 1791, in his "Report on the Coinage," Hamilton proposed an independent mint and currency for the United States on the basis of a bimetallic standard of gold and silver. There were no metallic deposits in this early America; minting coins would have meant the recoining of foreign specie. This movement was slow, and foreign coins continued to circulate in the United States until the Civil War. Nevertheless, the creation of a bimetallic standard placed America, in effect, in the gold area to which both Britain and Holland, the world's leading trading nations, belonged.

Manufactures. In December, 1791, Hamilton's greatest state paper appeared, his "Report on the Subject of Manufactures." True, Congress took no steps to carry out his recommendations; but to later generations, in America and abroad, his Report became the classical text on the relations of government and industry. Hamilton was casting a wider net than the protectionism with which his name has always been associated. Like Adam Smith—and he leaned on Smith heavily in all his Reports—he was dedicated to that "system of perfect liberty" in which men, as enterprisers, made free choices and in which nations survived and prospered because they cultivated those "peculiar advantages" that natural resources, habit, and skills helped them develop. All this would lead to "an increase of national industry and wealth"; it would augment "revenue [*income*] and capital"; this, in short, was the key to economic welfare. Such was the case for free enterprise and an international community based on the mobility of trade, labor, and capital. (*See Document No. 8.*)

Hamilton, however, was a realist and a patriot. Such a world did not exist; other nations were not only supporting their home industries but also discriminating against foreign products. America—a young nation, poor in capital, still wanting in skills—had to protect itself against such discrimination and, in the interests of defense, stimulate its own manufactures. Government intervention was, therefore, imperative, and Hamilton proposed all sorts of devices to speed this—protective tariff duties, prohibitive rates, bans on the export of raw materials, premiums and bounties. Hamilton, interestingly enough, favored the last: bounties could be used as temporary devices, they were more flexible than duties, there was little danger of their fostering monopolies. It was in his plea for the protection of "infant industries" that Hamilton was most imaginative and most persuasive. And he has been followed all over the world because such protection has appealed to new countries and is needed for defense.

In the Report, Hamilton's mind ranged freely over all aspects of the economy. America should encourage manufactures because a diversified economy was safer than one founded on the production of agricultural staples exclusively. Such an economy, too, increased the nation's "revenue and wealth." It would furnish more opportunities for employment; immigration would increase. Finally, foreign capital—and of this Hamilton spoke again and again—would be attracted to the United States.

The Congress turned a deaf ear to Hamilton's argument; and while the United States began to experiment with protective tariffs, in the 1830s, it was not until 1861 that America seriously turned its attention to industrialization. From 1861 to 1933, Hamilton's influence on American public policy was profound.

Public Lands. The devising of a public land policy was an integral part of Hamilton's fiscal program. He did not set it up; but he administered it to produce revenues. In 1785, the Land Ordinance laid out a land system that continued until almost the end of the 19th century. The public lands were to be sold at public auction, with the minimum knockdown price $1.00 an acre, payable in cash. These provisions were subsequently changed: later, squatters were permitted to settle and their pre-emption rights were protected. Although large land companies did enter the public domain, frequently for speculative purposes, the point nevertheless must be noted that small operating farmers were able to get on the land.

The Jay Treaty. One of Hamilton's outstanding triumphs was the effecting of a settlement with Britain. This was accomplished in 1795 with the Jay Treaty;

there is no doubt, however, that the treaty was due to Hamilton. The United States assumed the obligation of seeing that the old pre-Revolutionary debts owed English merchants were paid. In return, the English promised to evacuate the western posts and to pay damages for the seizures of American shipping in the war then raging between Britain and France. Most important was Britain's granting of equal trading rights to Americans in its home ports, although these rights did not extend to the West Indies; nor were promises given not to interfere with American shipping or impress American seamen. American neutrality, therefore, was in an uneasy status; but it was better than war—and war the United States stayed out of, thanks largely to Hamilton.

American Prosperity. What resulted was a period of unexampled business expansion, one of the greatest, in fact, the United States has had. Coming as it did at the beginning of its national career, it assured the success of the American political experiment. The American nation was securely established. The exports of the country mounted from $19 millions in 1791 to $93 millions in 1801. Imports stood at $29 millions in the earlier year and $111 millions in the later. Yet, despite an unfavorable balance of trade, payments on the foreign debt, and interest on foreign investments in the country, there is every reason to assume the balance of international payments was in the country's favor.

The American merchant marine was earning large sums in freights. Foreign capital—short-term and long-term—poured into the United States. In consequence, sterling exchange during the greater part of the period was selling at a discount in New York and Philadelphia; and the specie circulation of the country doubled, an evidence that foreigners were paying American balances in coin. It may very well be that the United States was a creditor nation—a position it did not re-achieve until 1915.

Hamilton again and again expressed the hope that foreign capital would appear to strengthen the American economy. It did: foreign capital was to be found in every area of American enterprise and in public finance. Thus in 1803, the first estimate we have available, of the $81 millions of federal debt outstanding, 53 per cent was held abroad; of the $48 millions of coporation stock outstanding, 33 per cent was in foreign hands. The Bank of the United States, capitalized at $10 millions, was owned by foreigners to the extent of 62 per cent.

Company promotions increased spectacularly. During the 1780's, only 33 chartered companies had been set up by the states; during the 1790s, the number of such new companies was 295. By 1800, there were in the country 34 banks, 33 insurance companies, and companies to further inland navigation, build and operate turnpikes and toll bridges, and water systems and docks. Manufacturing and mining, on a corporate basis, started only slowly. It was not until 1816 that such enterprises, commanding sizable capitals, were to appear.

Two sets of figures set off the impressive advances of this early period of Americn capitalism. With 1910-14 as the basis period of 100, the indices of wholesale prices stood at 86 in 1789, 146 in 1796, and 182 in 1814. The tonnage of American ships in the foreign trade increased from 123,893 tons in 1789 to 981,019 tons in 1810. The United States indeed was the land of opportunity. (*See Document No. 9.*)

— 5 —

PRE-INDUSTRIAL CAPITALISM

Merchant as Capitalist.   A key to the capitalist development of the United States before the Civil War is to be found in the fact that business enterprise was still largely in the mercantile stage. The businessman was a merchant, usually an undifferentiated one, who combined the functions of trader, "manufacturer," banker, and speculator. It was inevitable that foreign commerce should loom large at this time; and, in fact, through the operations of the import-, export-, and carrying-trades, the United States was able to balance its payments and so attract foreign capital into America.

"Manufacturing" for the most part was at the cottage, or domestic, stage of production. The workers usually were farmers; they labored in their own homes and furnished their own simple tools; they finished the manufactured goods from raw materials or partially-processed ware furnished them by the merchant-manufacturers. The latter then sold the finished articles. The workers, on their part, were frequently paid in goods, or truck, from the stores of the merchants. In this way, a good deal of the crude linen and woolen goods, straw hats, brooms, iron nails, boots and shoes of this early America was fabricated.

Foreign Trade. The golden period of the American carrying trade lasted from the founding of the Republic until the mid-1830s. Before the Napoleonic Wars were over, the tonnage of the American merchant marine stood at 1,500,000 tons, and American ships were to be found in every harbor of the globe. American seamen and merchants were resourceful: they participated in the rich China trade, opening a series of triangular voyages that took them to the northwest coast of North America (for otter furs), to Hawaii (for sandalwood), and thence to China (for spices, tea, silks, and chinaware); they engaged in trading voyages through the whole Indian Ocean; they hunted whales as far as the South Pacific. This was the day of the wooden sailing ship and American shipbuilders were the leaders of the world. The great profits American merchants made from all these activities came home to Boston, Salem, New York, and Philadelphia to sustain the trade with Britain in manufactured wares and for investment in the New England cotton industry and in the canals and early railways of New England, New York, and the Middle West.

By the mid-1830s, American pre-eminence in the China trade was slipping. From 1843 to 1857, thanks to the building of the clipper ships in Yankee yards, and the opening up of Australia and California (gold was discovered in both places), American shipping for another brief period became important. But with the outbreak of the Civil War, it was plain that America's destiny no longer was to be found on the high seas. Thus, in 1826,

92.5 per cent of foreign trade entering and leaving American ports did so in American bottoms; in 1860, the ratio had fallen to 66.5 per cent.

There were important reasons for this decline—and for the shifts of American capital to internal improvements and manufacturing. Iron had come in to replace wood, and the English were the great fabricators of iron (and steam) ships; English government subsidies made possible the establishment of lines running on schedule, across the Atlantic and the Indian Oceans; the eating of fish began to decline, in Europe notably, with improved diets and higher incomes; finally whaling was fated to disappear almost entirely as voyages lengthened and as coal oil and gas and then petroleum products began to supplant whale oil for illumination and lubrication.

Products in the Trade. While these developments were occurring, the articles entering foreign trade also changed markedly. Tobacco, fish, naval stores, furs, rice, and wood products had been the staples of the colonial trade; by the opening of the Civil War, cotton from the South and flour, wheat, and meat products from the Middle West were America's leading exports. So important had cotton become that, by 1860, American shipments overseas totaled almost 4 million bales and made up half of the value of the country's exports. Cotton, indeed, was king. Now New York City rose to prominence as America's leading port, for New York bankers and merchants financed the cotton trade and the purchases of cotton growers in Europe. In return for these exports, America bought its manufactured goods in Europe (metals and finished ironware and textiles) and its tea, coffee, and sugar from semi-tropical countries.

Balance of Payments. An analysis of the transactions entering into the country's international account points up the mercantile aspects of American capitalism at this time. During the three decades 1821-49, the value of imports exceeded that of exports by $150 millions; interest paid out came to $204 millions while new capital investments totaled $165 millions; immigrants brought in $86 millions, but American tourists spent $95 millions abroad. The great balancing factor in all these transactions was the carrying trade: the net earnings of freights and ships sold came to the impressive figure of $432 millions. As a result, despite business recession in the late 1810s and prolonged depression during 1837-43, European confidence in America continued and new capital flowed into the United States.

From 1850 to 1873, the components in the balance of payments changed sharply. Because of war needs and the beginnings of the processes of industrialization, American imports mounted sharply. (But the 1870s were the last decade to see the United States with an adverse trade balance.) The excess of merchandise imports over exports came to $1,500 millions. On the other hand, net freight earnings and ship sales almost disappeared, the balance in America's favor being only $250 millions. Immigrants brought in $330 millions to be more than offset by tourist expenditures of $576 millions. Interest paid to foreign investors totaled $904 millions against net capital investments from abroad of $1,000 millions.

What sustained the American economy? Curiously enough, gold; for the heavy gold production of California made possible the shipment of the metal of $1,116 millions during the years 1850-73! Foreign investments, because of the solvency of the United States, therefore could mount and the first great trunk railways spanning the continent could be financed with foreign, largely English, borrowings. In 1853, foreign investments in the United States stood at $222 millions; by 1869, these had risen to $1,465 millions.

Internal Improvements. As immigrants and native-born Americans poured westward to take up land and grow the staples of wheat, corn, and meat products in the North and cotton in the South, internal improvements both preceded and followed the settlers. The federal government started the process with the construction of the great Cumberland Road in 1806; located on the Potomac River as its eastern terminus, this highway extended across the Middle West. Those natural arteries of travel and trade, the river systems of interior America, also came to be utilized heavily. First, keelboats and flatboats and soon (after 1809) steamboats quickly made their appearances so that the Mississippi and its tributaries were thronged with the commodities of America moving out to sea. River towns became important—Pitts-

burgh, Wheeling, Cincinnati, St. Louis, New Orleans—
as mercantile and banking centers, and eastern capital
flowed west, too, to finance many of these operations and
to engage heavily in urban real-estate developments. (*See
Document No. 10.*)

Canals. The construction of canals was the inevitable next step, for canals tied the interior waters together
and brought western America to the eastern seaboard.
The first great canal, the Erie Canal (begun in 1817 and
completed in 1825), was sensationally successful. It was
financed by public issues of the State of New York
(largely purchased by English investors); and this pattern was quickly followed everywhere in the United
States. Pennsylvania, New Jersey, Ohio, Indiana—and
western states like Illinois and Michigan as well as most
southern states—at once launched upon elaborate projects of internal improvements with public financing.
Canal-building was their chief interest, but the programs
also included bridge construction, public banks, and even
railroads.

As a result, the American states went heavily into debt,
vastly overexpanded their public works, and the inevitable
day of reckoning that set in seriously hurt American
credit. In 1820, the indebtedness of the American states
was virtually nothing; in 1842, the total of such obligations stood at $200 millions. By 1837, the bubble of
speculation—in land and public works—was pricked,
depression set in, and the states resorted to defaults of
interest and some even to repudiation of principal. Foreign investors lost $40 millions by such defaults and
repudiations.

Railroads. Early experiments with railroads took
place under mixed auspices. Initially, many were started
as local enterprises, serving limited markets, and were
financed with general subscriptions. The lines in consequence were short and it was not until 1850 that Albany
and Buffalo were joined by the tying together of almost
a dozen such ventures. Public financing was more
important. The Baltimore and Ohio, the first trunk railroad, received large grants from Maryland; the Western
Railroad of Massachusetts also was state-financed; many
of the western and southern railroads were started off
in this fashion.

Greatest public contributor was the federal government. Early, it had begun to use land grants as a device to speed public improvements: swamps were drained, public schools were erected, and beginning with 1850, railroads were assisted. In this year, the states of Illinois, Mississippi, and Alabama were given some 2,500,000 acres of land right down the backbone of the continent to be held in trust for the builders of the Illinois Central Railroad. Illinois granted a charter; and into this company poured Eastern and English capital to build 700 miles of railroad at a cost of $16,500,000. The public lands attracted the subscribers and well they might for at least $25 millions were realized from their sale. The Illinois Central in time became one of America's great enterprises, justifying the confidence of investors who were willing to take risks as the new land grew. (*See Document No. 11.*)

Manufacturing. In only one area, in this period before the Civil War, did enterprise take on the characteristics of industrial capitalism, with sizable investment in mechanical operations and a wage-earning laboring class, and this was cotton textiles. As early as 1791, a spinning mill had appeared in Pawtucket, R.I.; but it was not until 1816 that large-scale automatic operations in both spinning and weaving made their appearance. Such factories, in the proper sense of the term, appeared in Waltham first, and then in Lowell, Manchester, and Lawrence; they spread into Maine, as well. Large companies, capitalized for as much as $1 million, employed young women for the most part as operatives. Wages were low and hours of work long, but a curious kind of philanthropy—indeed, it was early welfare capitalism —kept these workers contented as they lived in company dormitories and were encouraged to participate in amateur literary exercises. (*See Document No. 12.*)

Because capitalism was still pre-industrial, working class organizations were social, political, and fraternal bodies and they were interested in co-operative colonies rather than in collective bargaining and the improvement of working conditions. So-called unions did make their appearance (usually local in character); strikes broke out—but never were successfully concluded. It was not until the 1850s that the modern-day union made its appearance. Appearing among printers, hat-finishers, stone cutters, it was organized nationally and it put the accent of its activities on wage and hour bargaining.

Thus, American capitalism scarcely approximated its contemporary aspects. It handled and financed trade; it engaged in land speculation and town-lot jobbing; it participated in internal improvements; but it did not concern itself significantly with production. The high standards of living of this early America were to be associated with the paucity, or absence, of a labor reserve, and the well being of northern and middle-western agriculture. Accumulation took place, but, interestingly enough, such private wealth (except in cotton textiles) was not utilized to found industrial production. Iron and steel, oil refining, machinery and machine tools, and meat packing grew up from small beginnings and with no large-scale capital help from the merchants of the period. Perhaps this was better so; for while beginnings were modest, they represented the enterprise and daring of their innovators, who were at the same time the owners-managers.

Cotton Planting.   Curiously enough, it was in cotton planting, under the slavery system that the usual relations of capitalism were to be found. The cotton plantation, like the tobacco plantation before it, was linked with capitalist production in the modern sense. Capital was invested in slaves rather than in land (for land in the South was plentiful); credit was employed to make and finance the crop and the planter; and the staple produced entered world markets to be affected by supply and demand. With the development of textile industries everywhere, the demand for cotton regularly rose, and as it did, cotton planting expanded, moving across the South Atlantic and Gulf States into Arkansas and Texas by the time the Civil War broke.

Cotton production grew from 150,000 bales in 1815 to 4,500,000 bales in 1859. In the earlier year, almost all of the country's cotton was raised in the Old South; by 1859, only one-fourth of the crop was grown there and Mississippi alone was producing as much. Cotton prices, meanwhile, had varied sharply. In 1815, middling cotton was selling for 30 cents a pound; then it had begun to drop, reaching the low of 6 cents in 1844.

In 1850, cotton was selling at 12 cents, and during 1855-60, at 11 cents. Planters located in the rich alluvial lands of the Gulf area and the southern Mississippi Valley could carry on quite well at such a price; but, in the 1850s, Southern agriculture generally had fallen on hard times.

Costs of Southern Agriculture. The problem of the South was its complex structure of costs in a period of rising prices. Prices began to rise at the end of the recession of 1837-43 and did so sharply after 1850, as a result of the impact of the gold discoveries. Farm necessaries—implements, construction materials—went up; as did home necessaries; so did the costs of freight, commissions, insurance, and credit. Most alarming of all, was the rise in the cost of Negroes during the 1850s. The result was, Southern cotton was caught in the characteristic scissors of a growing spread between prices received and prices paid; and the South became more intransigent.

The Negroes. In the slave-holding states by 1860, there were some 8 million whites and some 4 million blacks, almost all of whom were slaves. Only some 2 million whites lived in slave-owning families; and even among this minority there was heavy concentration. If we regard 20 and more slaves as a large plantation, we find only 3 per cent of the white population (231,370 persons) living in such a unit; and they possessed considerably more than 50 per cent of the enslaved Negroes. Yet, the whole South (with minor areas of rejection) accepted the slave institution: for psychological, social, and economic reasons.

The slave was largely a field hand, for he represented capital; relatively few Negroes, therefore, were house servants or plantation mechanics. The South preferred to buy its requirements in the market, and sought a maximum cash return from the labors of its Negroes.

In 1808, under the Constitution, the African slave traffic had been outlawed; true, slave running and smuggling continued until about 1840, and then the South began to depend wholly on domestic supply. It is difficult to say that there was a conscious breeding of Negroes for sale; the fact is, however, that a large domestic trade sprang up, with Negroes moved from Virginia,

South Carolina, Kentucky, and Missouri, into the new South of the Gulf and the Southwest. As demand for Negroes increased and supply diminished, after the middle 1840s the price of Negroes went up. During 1820-60, almost a million blacks were moved from the old and border South to the lower South and Southwest; and these for the most part went with the traders in Negroes rather than with migrating planters.

Costs of Negroes. The prices of Negroes were based on those of the prime field hand, that is, the male Negro between the ages of 18 and 30 years; the average price, therefore, was between 40 and 50 per cent of that of the field hand. Again, the field hand's price was at about six to eight times of his annual rate of hire. Prices for field hands fluctuated until the middle 1840s, and then they rose steadily. In 1800, a field hand was being sold at $300; during 1808-10, at $900; in 1812, at $300; in 1819, at $1100. Prices dropped during the recessions of the 1820s and the 1830s. In 1845, the price was $600 and from thence on prices went up until, in 1860, field hands were selling at between $1200 and $1800. This advance reflected growing stringency in supply. At the same time, the ratio of cotton prices to Negro prices fell off sharply. The ratio is expressed in cents per pound of cotton to hundreds of dollars for the average slave: 1805, 4 to 1; 1819, 2 to 1; 1837, 1 to 1; 1860, 0.6 to 1.

A number of factors affected supply. The shutting off of the illegal African trade and the ability of Southwestern planters to pay more were important considerations; more and more, too, Negro slaves were being employed in industrial and other activities—railroad construction and operation, iron-manufacture, tobacco manufacture, cotton-textile manufacture, coal mining, lumbering, etc. Such Negroes, frequently, were hired, and this in turn affected prices of slaves.

Two comments are in order, here. It has been too frequently assumed that slave labor was inefficient labor and that it was ultimately incapable of competing with free labor. The facts are these, however: Negro slaves were being used in semi-skilled and even skilled occupations, with no loss of productivity; and later, when cotton came to be grown under the sharecropping system, after the Civil War, the yield per acre, or productivity, did not improve. The pinch came not as a result of the type of labor being employed, but because of its cost, that is, the capital cost.

It is for this reason that in the 1850s, particularly from the Old South, came the demand for the re-opening of the African slave trade. It was being said that Negroes in Africa could be had for $50, and in Virginia they were being sold at $1000 to $2000. The South obviously could not unite on this point, for the Border States and Virginia had become the breeding states. (*See Document No. 13.*)

The Direct Trade. The slave economy also began to find itself under another pressure, and that was the additional costs resulting from the movement of cotton and home and plantation necessities through New York. The New York merchants had become the factors, commission men, and bankers for the South; their charges and their inability, from time to time, to finance and protect the whole Southern cotton crop, made Southerners feel their disadvantage. Hence, the Southerners began to press for direct trade with England: shipping that would run from Liverpool to Southern ports, banks located in the South that would deal directly with Southern needs, and English wares that would be laid down at Southern docks instead of moving first by way of New York.

Tariffs. To Southerners, direct trade and free trade were two sides of the same shield. In fact, on the question of protectionism, after 1832, the Southerners had their own way. True, Henry Clay and the Whigs (the successors of the Federalists) pressed for protection as a part of their so-called American System. The American System called for support of internal improvements —thus opening up the whole nation's resources and markets; for protection—which would encourage infant in-industries in the North and the South, and in the latter diversify the capital fund; and for sound money and banking—which would encourage accumulation. But Clay failed on all points. The strength of the Democratic party in the country's politics after the 1830s prevented that internal reconstruction that might have spared America the Civil War.

The tariff is a case in point. The tariffs of the 1790s

were revenue tariffs; the tariff of 1816 was mildly protectionist, with 25 per cent the rate on cotton and woolen textiles. The tariffs of 1824 and 1828 raised schedules somewhat higher. The South was indignant, talked of nullification, but after 1833, duties were pushed down. The Whigs tried once more, in the Tariff Act of 1842, to raise rates, but from 1846 on, when revision downward began, the Southern view prevailed. In 1857, the country was almost on a free-trade basis. But now, a firm opposition had appeared in the person of the Republican party. Among other things, it spoke for the united industrial interests of New England, Pennsylvania, and the Middle West; and it demanded protection. The Republican party platform carried such a plank. It was no accident that in 1861, in the midst of the Civil War, the country's first real protective-tariff law was written.

Money and Banking. Another fundamental center of controversy between North and South was to be found in the nature of the money supply and the banking institutions of the country. A growing country or section will be pressed constantly for funds; at the same time, because it produces staples, it will seek to maintain high-price schedules. In consequence, it will be inflationary and willing to experiment with all sorts of devices that will ease credit. A central banking system that will control the money supply—through rigorous supervision over local banks, insisting that they remain on a specie basis—naturally is resented and resisted.

The charter of the First Bank of the United States had been permitted to lapse in 1811; but the Second Bank of the United States was chartered in 1816, also for 20 years. After 1823, when Nicholas Biddle became its president, the Bank began to run into storms. It assumed the role of a central bank, and in its ability to regulate domestic exchanges, it sought to expand and contract bank credit; also, it made efforts to check the flow of funds into land speculation, for this was playing a disproportionate part in the country's economy and utilizing funds that should have been available for mercantile and industrial needs.

Now South and West turned against the Bank, and the Bank's charter was not renewed after the bitter election campaign of 1832 gave President Jackson a popular mandate to terminate it. The result was that, from 1837 to 1863, state banking alone existed in the United States. In New York and New England, banks were supervised and therefore banking was sound. Not so in the South and West (except for Louisiana); here "wild-cat" banking generally reigned because of the demands for easy money and the clamors of land speculators. As a rule, many of these banks were only banks of issue, and an uncontrolled inflation set in because their notes were not on a specie basis. The depression of 1857 was, in very considerable measure, caused by this unsound banking system.

Business Crises.   American business, in large part, continued good during the period of the Napoleonic Wars, for American neutrality permitted the enormous expansion of the country's carrying fleet. Peace in Europe allowed Britain to challenge America on the seas and to expand manufacturing so that American markets could be flooded with English goods. There was a crisis in the United States in 1819, which continued for a number of years. From 1821 to 1825 revival took place; from 1826 to 1828, there was another short period of prosperity; there was revival again during 1830-33 and during 1834-37.

From 1837 to 1843, there was a sharp break in the American economy and this revealed the essential weaknesses of American business. Despite the growth in population, the push westward, and the increase in cotton cultivation, American accumulation and investment had no firm base. This could have been found only in manufacturing, but American enterprise was still mercantile and too much activity was speculative. The China trade was drying up; the English merchant marine was becoming increasingly competitive; land speculation was general—and risky. Overexpansion in land jobbing and internal improvements and the absence of central-banking control produced the crisis and depression which lasted into almost the middle of the 1840s.

From 1844 to 1857, American business again moved ahead, but irregularly and in short cycles of prosperity and decline. Funds once more flowed into the West into wild lands, bankrupt railways, and timber and mineral rights. The crisis of 1857 produced another setback and led to a re-examination of America's fundamental purposes.

Program for Industrial Capitalism. It was becoming apparent that the emphasis on trade and speculation could not permit America to weather storms and to grow. Land speculation and public works in sparsely settled areas led to failure sooner or later. American traders depending upon international markets were at the mercy of forces they could not control. An unsound banking system was a hindrance, in the long run, for the new manufacturing beginning to appear received little help. A program began to emerge which would sharply change the economy. This included protective tariffs for infant industry, a well-established banking system capable of assuring sound money, an adequate industrial labor supply, and an expanding domestic market. For this last, at least two conditions were required: easier access by agriculture to the public domain (by a homestead system, or free land entry) and federal support of trunk-line railroad construction.

This was the broad scheme which the new Republican party espoused. Many of these intentions were incorporated into the Republican party platform of 1860. The defeat of Southern slavery in the Civil War made possible the carrying out of the program; industrial capitalism then was launched in the United States and moved ahead to its great successes of capital accumulation and higher standards of living generally. The period 1861-1900 was one of impressive growth.

— 6 —

INDUSTRIAL CAPITALISM

Foundations for Industrial Construction. It was during the Civil War that the basis for the industrial growth of the United States was laid. Periods of war stimulate enterprise: the insatiable needs of armies in the field and ships at sea must be met; government finances itself by borrowings, and the monetization of debt enormously increases the money supply and, therefore, credit; fortunes are made and these are ploughed into new business promotions. So, during the war, the North found it necessary to float $2600 millions in bonds and to issue $450 millions in greenbacks; it was also compelled to suspend specie payments late in 1861; prices more than doubled; all this encouraged speculation but it also furthered enterprise. It was during the war that new names in the capitalist world appeared— J. P. Morgan, Andrew Carnegie, John D. Rockefeller.

Tariffs. Government assistance was basic, as well. During the war, aid was rendered the business community and notably industrial capitalism through a series of positive actions taken by the Congresses in Washington that put the economy on a secure footing. Protective tariffs were pushed up again and again, presumably to create revenues, really to permit infant industries to appear and grow. Beginning in 1861 and continuing until 1864, rates were revised upward so that at the war's end the average rate on dutiable goods was 47 per cent as compared with 18.8 per cent in 1861. Wool and woolens, copper, coal, iron (and steel) became the chief interests of tariff-writers; for these commodities previously had been imported from abroad; and their support made possible the gigantic development of these industries.

So great were the revenues pouring in from customs'

duties that Treasury surpluses began to appear and, indeed, continued until 1890. Generous support, in consequence, was given to demands for the construction of public buildings, the improvement of rivers and harbors, and the modernization of the navy. Debt redemption was pushed, but not too far, for the money supply of the country was tied to the public debt.

Banking. With the end of the Second Bank (1836), there was no central authority to supervise banking. The "wild-cat" banks of the states, with their constantly inflationary tendencies, disordered business. An effort was made to put the nation's banks on a sounder footing. In 1863, a nationally supervised system was set up under which federal authorities might charter banks and restrict their purposes. In 1865, state-bank notes were outlawed by the imposition of an annual 10 per cent tax on them. In the case of the new national banks, the heart of federal control lay in the tying of notes to federal bonds, for notes could be issued only up to 90 per cent of the market value of the bonds banks held. Further, provision was made for the mobilization of reserves in so-called reserve cities.

The new system had obvious advantages in checking the activities of state banks and in linking the new notes with gold. But the banks could not expand with business requirements: they could not serve agriculture's needs for long-term (and, indeed, for working) capital; they could not pump credit into the country's economy as anti-recessionary measures (for, in time of decline, bonds would rise and the banks could earn more by selling them than by issuing notes against them); the accumulation of their reserves in the larger cities encouraged brokers' loans and, therefore, stock speculation. In short, while the change was salutory in many particulars, it neither created a central-banking system (which, through monetary policy, could affect both recessionary and inflationary tendencies) nor could it furnish farm credit. It was not until 1913-16 that these fundamental banking reforms took place.

Homesteading. The Homestead Act of 1862 further made entry into the public domain easy. Farmers without capital or credit had found it difficult to purchase public lands, despite low prices. Increasingly, they had been entering as squatters. The Homestead Act accepted these attitudes and gave a quarter-section (160 acres) free to all bona fide settlers who erected an improvement and established residence. A homesteader could commute his quarter-section into a pre-emption at once by paying $1.25 an acre; he could also acquire an extra quarter-section on the same terms.

Undoubtedly, much fraud attended these processes. There were many charges of land companies acquiring large tracts through the use of dummy entrymen. It is further true that more farmers bought land (usually because of accessibility to railroads) than acquired the free homesteads. But land continued cheap right up to 1900 and all these activities made possible the doubling of lands in farms from 1860 to the end of the century. The farmer's discontent during this period centered in the paucity of credit rather than in so-called land monopoly.

Pacific Railways. Only government assistance made possible the quick construction of trunk railways to span the whole continent. The pattern of such aid was laid down in 1850 in the chartering of the Illinois Central Railroad. In 1862, two federally chartered railroads were authorized to build from the Missouri River to the Pacific Ocean—the Union Pacific and the Central Pacific—and they were given generous grants from the public domain and lent money for each mile of road laid down. In all, during the 1860s and 1870s, four such Pacific railways were chartered, with land grants and loans. From 1850 to 1873, 158,000,000 acres of land were thus voted and loans came to $64,500,000. Gigantic frauds attended these operations, not only through the use of dummy construction companies and the entry of lands other than those granted, but as well in the failure to pay either principal or interest on the loans. Too, railroads were badly constructed and had to be rebuilt again and again. Granted all this, the consequence nevertheless was immense, for far in advance of settlement, communication lines were thrown across the continent to facilitate movement, extent the domestic market, and increase the production of cereals and meat for export to a growing and industrialized Europe. After 1873, American exports exceeded imports, making possible the stepping up of foreign borrowings; and this was achieved only as a result of the vast expansion of the country's farm surpluses. Something of the measure of the railroads' contribution will be noted from the increase of railroad mileage from 30,000 to 193,000 during 1860-1900.

The industrialization of the United States, during 1860-1900, was speeded up as a result of many factors: the growing domestic market (protected by high tariffs); the formation of capital out of the high profits made by business which were ploughed back into plant expansion; and the ability to pay for imports needed in the industrial processes and for interest on foreign investments because of the great surpluses of cotton, wheat and flour, and meat products America was able to send abroad.

Immigration. At the same time the admission of foreigners into the United States was eased. Contract laborers were permitted; an Immigration Bureau, federally controlled, provided the necessary inspection services; and all manner of agencies—western States, land-grant railways, humane societies—carried on a steady propaganda to encourage European emigration. By the 1870s, 280,000 immigrants were arriving annually, on an average; by the 1900s, 1,000,000 on an average, were coming in each year. Up to the 1890s, these largely moved west to seek farms; from 1890 to 1914, the nature of the immigration changed, its chief sources being the countries of southern, central, and eastern Europe. The immigrants were entering the country's cities to add to its industrial reserve army.

From 1860 to 1896, real wages kept on increasing in the United States because of the advancing productivity and the relative dearth of industrial labor. From 1896 to 1910, this upward movement ceased, in considerable part due to the growth of the reserve army of labor fed from the two sources of European immigration and the movement from the countryside to the cities. A good deal of the unrest of the period can be ascribed to this development.

Evidences of Growth. In every area the country grew. Population doubled from 1870 to 1900. In 1870, only one-fifth of the American people lived in cities (places with 8,000 or more); in 1900, one-third. From

1860 to 1900, the size of the American farm domain doubled and the capitalized value of American farms increased from $8 billions to $20 billions. In 1860, the capital invested in American manufacturing was $1 billion; in 1900, this had grown to $10 billions. In 1860, the value of American manufactured products came to $2 billions; in 1900, this stood at $13 billions. At the same time, the number of wage-earners in manufacturing grew from 1,300,000 to 5,300,000. The impressive advances of the new industrialism were no better expressed than in the growth in production of basic raw materials and semi-processed goods.

PRODUCTION IN AMERICA (in thousands)

	1860	1900
Anthracite coal (short tons)	9,620	60,418
Bituminous coal (short tons)	6,013	193,323
Crude petroleum (barrels)	500	57,071
Pig iron (long tons)	751	13,621
Crude steel (long tons)	10	10,640

During this period of unexampled expansion, the country's national income rose from $2,380 millions in 1850 to $19,360 millions in 1900. At the same time, the real income per head of the occupied population almost doubled, that is, from $787 to $1,388.

Captains of Industry. This was the work and the accomplishment of America's first generation of industrial capitalists who owned and managed their concerns, took risks, made enormous profits, and reinvested most of them in new and improved plants, the acquisition of raw materials, and the financing of market agencies. They were enterprisers, adventurers, and innovators, for the great forward strides of technology were possible only as the results of their risk-taking. There is no doubt they engaged in cutthroat and unfair means of competition; there can be no question that in many areas monopoly practices were developed. On the other hand, they lowered costs, reduced prices, and kept wages high.

To call these early leaders "Robber Barons" is less than fair, for in a single undifferentiated body are grouped the Wall Street plungers and manipulators, the despoilers of railroads and the land monopolists, with the industrial

innovators. There is no doubt that the easy morality of
the period (standards of deportment were equally low in
public life) accepted modes of business conduct that
would be unalterably rejected today. There is no question, too, that the absence of income-tax and inheritance
laws made possible the building up of enormous personal fortunes and the habits of extravagant living. Too
easily, one is ready to assume that private fortunes, however gained, and human exploitation went hand in hand.
It is true that low standards of living among groups of
workers of the country were to be found: in part, this
was due to the crowding of great urban centers just
springing up, in part to the meager wages workers starting as unskilled laborers (whether from Europe or the
countryside) were receiving. However, it should be noted
that real wages doubled during this early period of
growth; and that many of the leaders of enterprise came
from the company of the humble.

A good deal of the élan of this period notably is associated with the existence of opportunity—that talents
could obtain recognition, that small capitals when successful could grow, that innovation at once obtained
recognition. It will be useful to see how typical enterprisers, starting obscurely, were able to build great industries and at the same time private fortunes. (*See
Document No. 14.*)

Andrew Carnegie. Andrew Carnegie had become
interested in iron during the Civil War when he was
superintendent of the western division of the Pennsylvania Railroad. He continued his activities with the war's
conclusion. In 1870, to supply his ironworks, he constructed his first blast furnace; in 1873, he and his partners organized their first steel company with a capitalization of $700,000, of which Carnegie held $250,000. Five
years later, in the midst of depression, the Carnegie Company was recapitalized at $1,250,000 with Carnegie him-
self owning 59 per cent of the stock.

As steel grew with the country, so did the Carnegie
activities. The company was owned by a partnership,
recourse to public financing never took place, and funds
for expansion were obtained from undistributed profits.
Using its own financial resources entirely, in the 11 years
1889-1900, the Carnegie Company was able to increase

annual steel production from 322,000 tons to 3,000,000 tons. Costs were constantly pushed down through technical innovation; but so were prices. In 1875, the average monthly cost of making steel rails was $57 per ton; the price received at the works was $66.50. In 1888, the cost was $28 and the price was $29.83. Carnegie was in favor of tariff-protection for his industry; he participated in pools; he sought railroad rebates. But success was associated with skilful management rather than through monopoly practices.

Profits steadily mounted and were employed for expansion, not only in the construction of additional blast furnaces but in the acquisition of coking ovens and iron deposits. By the former, he associated H. C. Frick with himself; by the latter, he bought heavily into the Mesabi iron range and at the same time linked railroads and steamship companies with his iron, coal, coke, limestone, furnaces, and mills. The end of the depression of 1893-96 saw the Carnegie Company the largest heavy-steel producer in the country. Profits mounted annually from $1,625,000 in 1880 to $40,000,000 in 1900. In this latter year, the recapitalization of the company was put at $320,000,000, all of it real—five hundred times the worth of the original investment of 1873. When the United States Steel Corporation was formed in 1901, the Carnegie Company's properties were valued at $492,000,000. The impressive Carnegie benevolences were set up from Carnegie's share of the sale and merger.

John D. Rockefeller. John D. Rockefeller and his partners organized their first company for the refining of oil with a capitalization of $1,000,000. In 1882, the Standard Oil Trust had a book value of $70,000,000. In 1889, when Standard Oil Company (New Jersey) was reorganized as a holding company, the net value of its properties was put at $196,713,000. In 1911, when the company was ordered dissolved by the Supreme Court, its net value had grown to $660,452,000. Profits were reinvested—into plant, equipment, research, the acquisition of marketing companies and foreign subsidiaries—and not distributed wholly (almost one-half of net earnings were treated in this way.) The result was, Standard Oil, starting in refining and transportation, was able constantly to improve its processes of manufacturing and

distribution as it extended into oil fields and foreign
markets.

Unlike Carnegie, Rockefeller could not escape criti-
cism and investigation. Carnegie had formed a vertical
integration in steel which dominated its field as completely as did Standard Oil that of oil. But Standard
reached large numbers of people—the independent small
producers of petroleum whose products it bought and the
vast consumer market of kerosene which it served at
retail through its own distributing machinery. In consequence, Standard Oil became the symbol of "monopoly": to be exposed, investigated, sued, and proceeded
against by public authority.

Regulation.   Malpractices by railroad managers and
the growth of bigness in business led to a growing popular
demand for regulation. Public intervention, taking the
form of assistance and encouragement to business, was
as old as the Republic itself; intervention to restrict and
control business, however, was new. As a result of
agrarian discontent and the protests of small businessmen,
Congress intervened to regulate and control first in 1887
when the Interstate Commerce Act was passed and then
in 1890 with the Sherman Antitrust Law. True, in the
beginning, neither law was particularly effective. It was
not until 1913, for example, that the Interstate Commerce Commission was given the power to make a
financial valuation of railroad properties as the first step
in the process of regulating rates. And as regards the
Sherman Act, it was not until 1911 that the Supreme
Court ordered the dissolution of a group of large companies on the ground that they used "unreasonable"
methods to restrain competition. (*See Document No.
15.*)

Recessions and Recoveries.   In an economy so vola-
tile and with many speculative elements in it, it was to be
expected that the course of business should have sharp
ups and downs in it. The absence of monetary and fiscal
mechanisms for affecting recession and inflation was a
fundamental flaw; but America's heavy dependence upon
European markets for credit and outlets for its farm surpluses also played an important role. The Civil War had
led to a sharp rise in prices, and it was not until 1878 that
prices once more were restored to their 1860 levels. From

thence on, wholesale prices dropped steadily until by 1896 they had declined 25 per cent. Price movements were not uniform, falling most sharply in wheat and flour, textiles, and iron and steel. The tapering off of gold production throughout the world may have had something to do with price decline; so did contraction of government expenditures; but most important was the lowering of costs due to technology and superior management. (*See Document No. 16.*)

The years 1873-79 saw sharp depression in the United States, as foreign funds became tight and securities were dumped in the American market. American rails had speculatively overbuilt and this was a source of weakness. Railroads went into default and railroad construction ceased; the unemployed reached at one time a total of 3 million; immigration slowed down; and there was widespread vagrancy and serious industrial conflict. But recovery, when it came, was pronounced, and the country continued its upward climb. By 1883, when the boom again was in full swing, new railroad construction came to 11,600 miles.

The tale of recession was repeated during 1893-96, with Europe once more bringing its dislocations into America. The collapse of the London banking house of Baring Brothers led to the tightening of credit extended to America and the sale here of large quantities of European-held securities. The American banking system was inadequate in the face of pressures, country reserves were withdrawn from banks in the central reserve cities, the stock markets suffered severe blows. Railroads again were hard hit and by 1895, 156 railroads, operating 39,000 miles of track, were in receivership. More than 600 banks and loan companies, among them 158 national banks, closed their doors. Agriculture was particularly hard hit, seeing its difficulties, and rightly, in declining prices and tight credit. It called for more money as a solution and raised the standard of "free silver":— a simplified remedy for complicated difficulties.

The United States was on a bimetallic standard, but little silver was being minted because of silver's overvaluation (due to heavy mining of the metal). The Silver Purchase Act of 1890 permitted a nominal minting of silver, but to many even this was too much. The Treasury called for the repeal of the law, this was done in 1893, but the drain of gold out of the country continued. Bond sales to build up the gold reserve were unavailing and it was not until 1896, when the recession burnt itself out, that business began to improve. The defeat of Bryan in the campaign of 1896; the rise in prices; bank credit expansion—all these heralded good times once more. The ghost of silver was laid once and for all in the Currency Act of 1900, which established the gold standard and made provision for a Treasury reserve fund of $150 millions.

Thus America grew under the leadership of its first generation of industrial capitalists. Its great expansion economically brought large benefits to the country and to almost every sector of the population. At the same time, distortions and inequities were appearing; and these were to receive mounting attention during the next decade and a half.

— 7 —

THE NEW FREEDOM

Distortions in Society. An economy characterized by advances and sudden changes inevitably produces distortions and dislocations. No society can endure for long where inequities continue to exist; yet, inequities are very likely to occur in early periods of dynamic growth. Social protest, in consequence, does not necessarily mean that fundamental faults have developed which can be rectified only by revolutionary upheaval. By reform, in short, a society can be put back on the right track without disordering its fundamental purposes as long as all elements in the population accept the common commitment.

This was the case in the America of 1900-14. Generally, there was agreement that private property and private accumulation were the keys to America's well-being and that equality of opportunity did exist. On all sides, on the other hand, there were evidences of disequilibrium. Because of population pressures, great cities with inadequate housing and slums were springing up; childhood diseases (diphtheria) and early-youth diseases (tuberculosis) were taking heavy tolls. Women and children were inducted into the labor army, with women frequently working at night and with home work common. Hours of labor were long—60 hours a week was general, 70 hours a week existed in steel; industrial accidents, as a result, were heavy. The absence of income taxes and of a sense of social obligation encouraged the newly rich to erect gaudy mansions and engage in conspicuous consumption in entertainment, clothes, and social habits generally. The differences between rich and poor were striking. Nor did government assume responsibility for unemployables and the maladjusted; the programs of private philanthropy were not much further advanced.

When, to this scene of sharp contrasts, are added the slowing down in the growth of real wages, large unemployment during business recessions (1904, 1907, 1913-14), the existence of a great army of unskilled and migrating workers (in harvesting, lumbering, metal mining), agriculture's tardy recovery (notably in the South), and the general hostility on the part of business to recognize trade unions and bargain with them on hours and wages, explosive elements were present aplenty.

Concentration. The renewal of the processes of creating industrial and financial concentrations, notably during 1899-1904, alarmed Americans; little business appeared to be threatened. The passing away of the first generation of innovators, the desire to obtain the benefits of integration, the utilization of the money market (frequently for the first time) to permit of expansion into new processes were factors in encouraging combination. There is no doubt that financial promotion by investment bankers—with large promotional fees and overcapitalization of companies—also played its part in this merger movement. Great new corporations like United States Steel, United States Rubber, American Can, International Harvester appeared. The American public absorbed the securities of 79 large combinations with a capitalization of $4 billions.

According to John Moody, writing in 1904, there were in the United States 318 industrial integrations with a combined capitalization of $7.3 billions, 234 of which had sprung up during 1899-1904. Among them, there were ten giants each capitalized in excess of $100 millions. Into the bargain, many of the giants were mobilized as two great empires headed by J. P. Morgan, the investment banker, and John D. Rockefeller, whose interests ramified into coal and iron, steel, copper and lead, and banking.

Nor was this all: there was a similar concentration in money and banking. Great banks, allied with investment houses and insurance companies because they could control the investment of the country's savings, presumably dominated credit and proliferated into the industrial life of the nation. By interlocking directorates chiefly, a small company of men—so it was declared—could make all the significant business decisions of America. According to the Pujo Committee (1913), the financial houses associated with J. P. Morgan and Co. commanded financial resources totalling $2 billions; at the same time, the partners of the Morgan firm held 341 directorates in 112 corporations with a combined capitalization of $22.5 billions. (*See Document No. 17.*)

Organized Labor. The power of organized labor seemed puny by comparison. In 1900, out of some 15 million wage-earners, less than one million were organized in trade unions. In 1904, organized labor commanded some 2 million members, and in 1914, only 2.6 million. Most of these were in unions affiliated with the American Federation of Labor (formed 1886); and they preached a "voluntaristic" philosophy of improvement through collective bargaining. The closed shop, in consequence, was a key demand. But because these unions were largely on a craft basis, they were incapable of reaching the great masses of workers in the new integrations which performed on an industrial rather than on a craft level. Strikes were the weapon of the unions; but business fought back by injunctions (obtained from the courts) and not infrequently industrial warfare. (*See Document No. 18.*)

Revolutionary Labor. It was no accident that the activities of unskilled, migrating, casual workers, who fell outside this pattern, should take on a revolutionary cast. There were large numbers of these, frequently without homes and families, who followed temporary jobs in the great wheat fields of the west, as well as in its lumber camps and metal mines. They began to join the Industrial Workers of the World (formed 1905), which preached a revolutionary syndicalist program of working-class seizure of power directly. The I. W. W. disclaimed an interest in political action; it sought disruption through sabotage; it engaged in mass strikes; it fought for free speech. From 1905 to 1917, it was claimed, the I. W. W. issued one million cards to members; at no one time, however, did it possess more than 100,000 members. In 1912, the I. W. W. moved east to organize textile workers (largely foreign-born, where anarchistic ideas were familiar); and while its strikes were unsuccessful, it nevertheless had a real influence in dramatizing the problems and discontents of American workers.

Advances. All this having been said, when viewed in the large, the American economy continued to make great forward strides. Concentration, apparently, did not stultify innovation; and if investors, in the short run, suffered as a result of overcapitalization, before long business accomplishment squeezed the excess water out of companies' financial structures. The following figures show advances in a few key areas:

INDEXES OF PHYSICAL OUTPUT (1899 = 100)

Year	Agriculture	Manufacturing	Fuel Production	Metal Mining
1900	101	102	106	109
1915	125	218	226	212

In manufacturing alone, from 1900 to 1914, the capital invested per worker increased 80 per cent, the horsepower per worker 75 per cent, and the output per manhour, 50 per cent. Agriculture's position continued to improve slowly but steadily, the realized income of the country's farmers rising from $3.6 billions in 1905 to $5.9 billions in 1915. There was an increase in tenancy and credit costs remained high; but agriculture (outside of cotton) was becoming more efficient and obtaining higher yields from capital investment as it turned increasingly to mechanization, used fertilizer, and introduced blooded stock for dairying and meat production. Other important shifts were from beef to dairying and from wheat to corn—hogs.

This thriving, risk-taking, capitalist America experimented ceaselessly with new industries (where initial capitals were small) and revolutionized long-established ones through new investment based on technical research. These new industries, starting humbly and attended by frequent business failure, made their appearance during this period of critical examination: automobiles, motion pictures, radio. And these attracted large capital from the start and also came to flourish: cotton textiles in the South, electrical machinery and power, street transportation, and the electrification of cities. On the one hand, steel spent large sums in improvement, converting from Bessemer furnaces to the open-hearth method, installing more efficient coke ovens, learning to use scrap steel; and new "Little Steel" companies arose to challenge the power of United States Steel—Bethlehem, Inland, Jones-Laughlin. On the other hand, large concentrations as purchasers, developed a countervailing power to that of the sellers: in the mail-order business (Sears-Roebuck, Montgomery-Ward), the retail grocery business (Atlantic and Pacific), the variety-goods chain stores (Woolworth, Kress, Kresge). (*See Document No. 19.*)

Productivity. Presumably, the concentration movement did not check innovation, for not only did the gross national product increase but so did productivity (represented by manhours of labor). In terms of billions of 1929 dollars, as Frederick C. Mills has showed, the GNP increment increased $161 billions during the decade 1901-10 over that of 1891-1900; the labor input increment increased $85 billions; and the productivity increment increased $76 billions.

Demands for Reform. From many quarters and under diverse leaderships, the reform forces gathered to press for larger government intervention. Politics had to be cleaned up, "bossism" ended, and direct participation by the electorate encouraged through the initiative, referendum, and recall. The cities, with their slums, crime, and poverty, needed attention. Public responsibility for problems of health, dependency, industrial accidents, and unemployment had to be assumed. The ogre of "Big Business" had to be faced. Two contrary positions in this last connection emerged. Theodore Roosevelt (in part inspired by Herbert Croly's "Promise of American Life" published in 1909; in part by his own experiences as President when he had created the Bureau of Corporations) saw the need for large intervention by the federal government not so much to dissolve concentrations but to regulate them closely, notably their financial practices. Woodrow Wilson, late president of Princeton University and governor of New Jersey (his mentor was Louis D. Brandeis), expressed the fear that opportunity was dying for little business. His creed of "The New Freedom" (expressed in his campaign addresses in the Presidential contest of 1912) called for a return to the pristine values of small producers, modest fortunes, and individual responsibility. The people must rule their own economic life and not through trusteeship of great enterprises. Regulation was not enough; competition had to be restored.

Woodrow Wilson sought to carry out this program by tariff and banking reform, the amendment of the Sherman Antitrust Act, and improvement in the machinery of agricultural credit. Suffice it to say that, in the long run, it was Theodore Roosevelt and not Woodrow Wilson who correctly read the signs of the times; and that the New Deal of Franklin D. Roosevelt continued in the tradition of the New Nationalism of Theodore Roosevelt rather than in the New Freedom of Woodrow Wilson.

Tariff of 1913. The tariff law of 1913 revised sharply downward most of the rates in all its fourteen schedules. There were reductions on almost 1000 items; an over-all cut of 10 per cent from the average of duties of the Tariff Act of 1909 was installed. Protectionism still continued, but an effort was made to apply it closely to infant industries only. At the same time, the farmers' free list was increased widely. Of greatest significance was the incorporation in the act of an income tax law, which had been authorized through the ratification of the Sixteenth Amendment in 1913. A democracy to survive under the dispensation of free enterprise must constantly concern itself with redistribution of wealth and income. Increases in real wages and taxation effect such a purpose; and the New Freedom began the slow climb (vastly accelerated during 1935-57) toward this end.

Banking. The national banking system, while it had rectified many of the errors of exclusive state banking, had begun to demonstrate its inadequacies as early as the 1890s. By tying note issues to bonds, it had given the country an inelastic currency; its reserve system had not protected banks but had unduly encouraged stock-market speculation; it had done nothing for agricultural credit; and it lacked mechanisms (notably those of changing the rediscount role and permitting open-market operations) to control the booms and depressions of the business cycle. The United States, in short, had no central banking to affect monetary and fiscal policy; this, in part, the Federal Reserve Act of 1913 supplied. (Thoroughgoing changes to strengthen central-banking controls were written in the Banking Act of 1935.)

Under the aegis of a Federal Reserve Board of seven members (two of which were to be the Secretary of the Treasury and the Comptroller of the Currency, with the other five appointed by the President) there were to function 12 federal reserve banks established in 12 key cities. The currency of the country was to be federal reserve notes (in place of the bank notes of the former national banking system) and these were to be based on commercial and agricultural paper, when offered for discount. Reserves were to be mobilized in the federal reserve banks; a gold reserve of 40 per cent was to be maintained. The federal reserve banks were invested with the rediscount function, so that member banks were in a position to sell their commercial paper and government securities to these agencies. The reserve banks, in turn, by raising and lowering their rediscount rates—and the reserve requirements—could contract and expand the flow of commercial credit. To achieve the same purpose, the federal reserve banks (they were to do this through an open-market committee) were authorized to engage in open-market operations, largely the buying and selling of government bonds, which in turn would affect the ⸱sitions of member banks vis à vis private credit. ⸱ttention, also, was given to the needs of agriculture, for the rediscount period for agricultural paper was put at 6 months as against that of commercial paper at 3 months.

Antitrust Legislation. President Wilson was committed to the idea that "private monopoly is indefensible and intolerable." At his request, and to improve opportunities for enterprise, Congress passed in 1914 the Federal Trade Commission Act and the Clayton Antitrust Act (as an amendment to the Sherman Law).

The Federal Trade Commission Act abolished the Bureau of Corporations and replaced it by a new agency with investigative and regulatory powers. The FTC could conduct investigations on its own account or at the request of the President or Congress. As a regulatory body, it was empowered to declare "unfair methods of competition and commerce" illegal. Once, by hearings, it had determined that such unfair methods existed, it was empowered to issue "cease and desist orders," to be enforced by the federal courts. "Effective competition," in short, was to be re-established not through criminal or civil actions but by the force of exposure. However, if unlawful restraints of trade were involved, the government could act through the Sherman and Clayton Laws. The FTC became a busy agency in the Wilson Administrations and, during 1915-21, it issued some 379 "cease and desist orders." In 1920, it listed some of the practices it had outlawed, as follows: "Misbranding of fabrics and other commodities; adulteration of goods, bribery of buyers; payment of bonuses by manufacturers to salesmen of jobbers and retailers to push their goods; procuring business or trade secrets of competitors by espionage or bribery; the use of false or misleading advertising; threats to the trade of suits for patent infringements; misrepresentation in the sale of the stock of corporations; all schemes for compelling retailers and wholesalers to maintain resale prices. . . ."

The Clayton Act contained largely three distinct sets of provisions: (1) It prohibited certain corporate practices, particularly those that had to do with interlocking directorates in industrial corporations and banks. (2) It provided remedies for relief. (3) It excepted organized labor from the provisions of the Antitrust laws. The labor provisions of the Act were to be found in sections

6 and 20, section 6 being hailed as labor's "Magna Carta." This declared that "the labor of a human being is not a commodity or article of commerce; nothing contained in the antitrust laws shall be construed to forbid the existence and operation of labor, agricultural, and horticultural organizations."

Section 20 sought to protect workers from the indiscriminate use of the injunction by the federal courts, declaring that "strikes, picketing, peaceable assembly, boycotts, and the collection of strike benefits" were not in violation of federal law. In the 1920s, these devices failed; and it was not until the Norris-LaGuardia Injunction Law of 1932 that labor was given adequate defenses against legal abuses. Indeed, it was not until 1935, under the Wagner Labor Relations Act, that trade unions as collective bargaining agencies were recognized.

Helping Farmers. During much of 1870-1900, as prices descended, American farmers met hard times. Largely, their problem centered in the difficulties of obtaining credit to purchase land, stock, and equipment and to finance harvesting operations. It was inevitable that farmers and their spokesmen should tinker with monetary panaceas, for more money would ease debts and provide funds for expansion. Farmers, in consequence, were to be found in the forefront of the discontented and active in reform movements during the whole of this period. The first Wilson Administration finally gave attention to these farmer grievances in both the Federal Reserve Act and the Federal Farm Loan Act of 1916. Using the Federal Reserve System as a model, the Federal Farm Loan System set up 12 federal land banks which were to help finance the activities of cooperative farm loan associations and joint-stock land banks. Farmers could borrow up to 50 per cent of the value of improvements. Finally, in 1923, Congress rounded out this program when it set up the federal intermediate credit banks, to rediscount agricultural paper and to lend directly to farm cooperatives.

The Outbreak of War. The Wilson Administration sought to explore other fields of change, notably as regards the position and well-being of labor. But, by 1915, the United States was being increasingly involved in World War I as a neutral and as a large supplier (and creditor) of the Allied nations. From 1915 on, in fact, as the Allied powers were being permitted to raise funds directly in the American money market—thus overnight changing the status of the United States from a debtor to a creditor nation—the American economy was on a wartime footing. Production and employment increased, agriculture enjoyed prosperity, and wholesale prices almost doubled from 1916 to 1920. There was a sharp recession during 1921-22; and then there followed the "Prosperity Everlasting" of the 1920s.

— 8 —

BOOM AND COLLAPSE: THE 1920s

The Economic Progress of the 1920s. To every eye and on every hand, economic and social miracles were occurring in the America of the 1920s. The postwar recession of 1921-22 was short-lived; recovery was great as the United States proceeded to dismantle its military machinery and wartime controls and apply itself once more to the arts of peace. American strength was utilized to overcome the backlog of consumer demand, invest in new industries and the modernization of old ones, and pour great sums abroad—both in private investment and in the purchase of the public securities of foreign governments—to help the economic processes everywhere. There was full employment in almost every sector; demand for residential housing and consumer durables (automobiles, household appliances) seemed unceasing. Americans had cause for pride in the great contributions made by technological innovation and improved management which increased productivity so impressively; in the vast expansion of the use of electrical power; and in the development of assembly-line techniques which made possible the mass production of automobiles, radios, vacuum cleaners—in fact, an endless array of products. There were, at the same time, flaws in the economy—but these were to become known only in retrospect. In the 1920s, Americans marveled at these evidences of their accomplishment. (*See Document No. 20.*)

Signs of Accomplishment. The national income of the United States (in 1926 dollars) increased from $58 billions in 1920 to $71.7 billions in 1929. Net capital formation for nonmilitary purposes during 1919-30 came to $74.6 billions of which business contributed $44.8 billions, residential construction $14.7 billions, and government $15.1 billions. From 1920 to 1929, productivity per manhour in manufacturing went up 40 per cent, in mining 20 per cent, and in steam railroads 20 per cent. In manufacturing (1899 = 100) the horsepower index per wageearner went up from 270 to 370 in the same eleven years. Agriculture's advances were not as great, but they were impressive.

New Industries. The automobile came into its heyday, particularly after 1928 when Henry Ford's Model A was released. Automobile production increased from 573,000 vehicles in 1914 to 5.3 million in 1929— the United States was turning out 85 per cent of the world's motor cars and trucks. Endless experiment and frequent failures had attended the rise of this industry, for from 1903 to 1926, some 181 companies had appeared. Mergers and concentration then developed with Ford and General Motors responsible for 68 per cent of total production in 1929. With the automobile also came the hard-surfacing of roads and a whole host of new industries (dealers, garages, roadside stands, and tourist cabins) as Americans became a highly mobile people.

The radio also became important with the Radio Corporation of America the key company as a result of its acquisition of some 2,000 basic patents. In the five years 1921-26, sales increased from $4 millions to $60 millions; at the same time, broadcasting stations were being established all over the country (562 by 1924). In chemicals (producing new fabrics and new paints), in aviation, in motion pictures (sound took the place of films), in retail distribution (as chain stores vastly expanded), the same tale was to be told: new capital for financing, consolidations, branch plants, and outlets everywhere throughout the country.

If a single key is to be sought to dramatize these changes, it can be found in the electric power and light industry. Between 1902 and 1917, electric power output grew ten times and the revenue of power companies five times. Between 1922 and 1927 alone, the power generated in the country doubled. New financing helped; but it also brought in its train mergers and concentration of control through holding companies. By 1927, such great corporations dominated 77.4 per cent of installed capacity.

Mergers. A characteristic of the time was the reappearance of the combination movement. Between 1919 and 1929, nearly 7,000 firms disappeared as a result of mergers; between 1921 and 1928, some 1268 industrial combinations were organized—in iron and steel, oil, nonferrous metals, food manufacture, textiles, and retailing. In this last, by 1929, corporate chains controlled 10 per cent of all retail outlets and made 32 per cent of all the country's annual retail sales. So significant had great corporations become that one-tenth of the corporations in the country owned more than half of the nation's corporate assets. New security issues (for new firms, but increasingly to finance consolidations) were launched on the security markets: in 1922, such issues came to $2.4 billions; in 1929, to $8 billions. Investment bankers inevitably were playing larger roles in financing and in management. The same tendency that had appeared in the 1900s was evidencing itself in the 1920s. As a result of such mergers, by the end of 1929, 3 companies in the telephone and telegraph fields had securities outstanding with a market value of $4.4 billions; 11 companies in the electrical equipment field had securities outstanding valued at $2.3 billions; 23 companies in automobiles had securities valued at $2.6 billions; 25 companies in iron and steel were valued at $2.1 billions. (*See Document No. 21.*)

Role of Finance. There was no question that an unparalleled expansion of credit was taking place—in installment loans, business loans, stock-market loans, new security flotations, and foreign portfolio investments (foreign dollar bonds). The 1920s saw no causes for concern and regarded their effects as salutary. It was calculated that 13 per cent of all retail sales in 1929 were being financed through installment payments. The fact is, the whole nature of the banking business was being transformed. Whereas, in 1900, business loans accounted for one-half of the assets of banks, by the end of the 1920s these had dropped to 20 per cent. Banks more and more were turning to real estate, loans against securities (to finance broker loans), and consumer credit. Their own security portfolios were growing and, in fact, through affiliates many banks were in the investment banking business.

The Federal Reserve System had no effective checks on this expansionary process. It tinkered with the rediscount rate several times, but it was confronted by a dilemma: raising the rate might reduce brokers' loans (they came to as high as $8 billions in 1929) but such a policy would contract only further business loans. In fact, in 1927, the Board forced down the rediscount rate; it was accepting "cheap money" as basic policy. From then on, speculation and company promotions could not be checked; the country rushed on to disaster.

Plight of Agriculture.   There were serious flaws in the whole economy and these, by 1929, were having a cumulative effect. Monetary and fiscal policy was incapable of checking the speculative boom in securities, fed by the wave of mergers with accompanying overcapitalization of new corporate organizations. New technological and management advances brought no fundamental redistribution of the national income; it was true, quality was improving, but the stickiness of prices, particularly in heavy industry, led to a slowing down in the upward movement of real income for wage-earners. What was taking place, in effect, was a profit inflation, with funds thereby obtained moving more and more into capital investment but also into speculation and luxury spending. In addition, agriculture was in a bad way and the country's international transactions were the reverse of what health and growth required.

As a result of many forces at work—overexpansion during the war; the opening up of new grasslands the world over; changes in dietary habits; the shift from

cotton and woolens to synthetics; the displacement of
horses by tractors and trucks (and the decline in the
consumption of animal feeds); higher productivity of
agricultural machinery—American agriculture was in distress during the whole of the 1920s. The prices-received
to prices-paid index dropped from 100 in 1913 to 90 in
1929. Farm mortgage debt rose from $3.2 billions in
1910 to $9.7 billions in 1929; tenancy mounted; while
the index of land values declined (1912-14 = 100) from
170 in 1920 to 115 in 1930. Surpluses of wheat and
cotton, as well as other staples, piled up; farm mortgages
were being foreclosed; and farm purchasing power almost
disappeared from markets. Legislative programs of relief
either failed of passage or the little that was done was
unavailing. (*See Document No. 22.*)

Foreign Transactions. A bad imbalance appeared
in the country's economic transactions with other lands.
The United States, from 1915 on, had become a creditor
nation—on net account, more American capital was invested overseas than European capital was invested in
the United States. Normally, such a situation would
require the stepping up of imports; but the reverse was
occurring. During 1906-10, annual average, the export
gap came to $434 millions; during 1921-25, annual
average, it stood at $947 millions and during 1926-30,
at $744 millions. At the same time, American funds
were pouring overseas to earn interest, profits, and commissions. By 1930, American holdings—in direct investments and the portfolio investments of foreign governments and companies—came to $16 billions. But be-
cause earnings on these could not be returned to the
United States as imports, they had to be reinvested—
more and more in speculative foreign government and
company securities.

Public policy acted in reverse; instead of lightening
tariff burdens, it increased them. The tariff acts of 1922
and 1930 pushed schedules higher and higher, in 1922
the general average *ad valorem* rate standing at 33.2
per cent and in 1930 at 40.1 per cent. Reprisals followed,
particularly during 1930 and 1931, so that the depression of 1929 and after was deepened as a result of re-
taliatory measures against American goods taken by some
25 countries.

Position of Labor.   The mass consumers of the nation, its working populations, enjoyed only a small share of the new prosperity. Real wages improved, of course; according to Paul Douglas, the average annual real earnings of American workers rose from an index of 101 in 1914 to an index of 125 in 1926 (1890-99 = 100). But real earnings did not rise synchronously with productivity. Thus, in manufacturing, during 1923-29, productivity per manhour went up 32 per cent; but average hourly earnings went up only 8 per cent. In coal mining, productivity increased 4 per cent, while average hourly earnings dropped 14 per cent. (*See Document No. 23.*)

It has been said here, again and again, that social stability is linked with the equitable distribution of the social income. There were serious disparities in the America of the 1920s. According to the Brookings Institutions study, *America's Capacity to Consume* (1935), the following were family incomes and their shares of the national income in 1929. Families receiving $5,000 a year or better constituted 8.2 per cent of the country's family population, yet they received 42 per cent of the country's income. But families receiving $2,000 a year or less made up 59.5 per cent of the country's family population, and they accounted for only 23.7 per cent of the country's income.

Labor's failure to improve its lot in part was due to the short-sightedness of management and in part to its own weaknesses. Not all employers failed to see the relationship between mass consumer demand and general economic well-being; Henry Ford, for example, raised daily wages first to $5 and then $7. The absence, however, of organized power among the workers made it impossible for them to present their case. At the end of World War I, there were some 5 million workers in the trade union movement; in 1929, their numbers had dropped to 4 million. At the same time, so-called company unions grew to a membership of 1.5 millions. Strikes occurred in steel, coal, meat packing, and the rails; none was successful.

On the one hand, courts were permitting the use of injunctions despite the Clayton Act; management was penetrating unions through labor spies and winning workers away by profit-sharing and stock-purchase devices. On the other hand, trade-union leadership, sticking rigorously to its craft formula, was incapable of organizing the great mass-producing industries of steel, automobiles, rubber, and electrical supplies; at the same time, these union leaders flirted with management ideas by setting up banks, dabbling in real estate, and buying companies. Also, the AFL unions adhered to their notion of "voluntarism": they sought no social security legislation. And none was passed during the 1920s, so that workers were denied the fringe benefits of unemployment and health protection.

Boom and Collapse. From 1922 to 1929, wholesale prices remained stationary. During periods of boom, prices usually rise; and because they did not, commentators in the 1920s spoke of a "profitless economy." Exactly the reverse was the case. Corporate profits continued high—the highest in American annals to that time. The overall average of wholesale prices concealed sharp price drops in agriculture, cotton textiles, and bituminous coal; there was no prosperity here. At the same time the too high prices of iron and steel, cement, and chemicals did not reflect the great technological improvements that were taking place.

Profits did not bolster purchasing power; and in part they moved into the stock market. In 1925, the market value of all shares listed on the New York Stock Exchange was $27 billions; in October, 1929, their worth was $87 billions. How deep the depression sank may be noted from the fact that on March 1, 1933, this had dropped to $19 billions. For those who could read and understand such intelligence, danger signs appeared as early as 1928, when residential building fell off sharply; and the fall of 1929, when automobile and steel production began dropping off. The English money rate was raised to 6½ per cent; foreign short-term funds began to move out of the United States.

In October, 1929, the boom collapsed, and in two weeks stock prices fell as much as 80 per cent below their highs of September. Panic was followed by recession and recession by depression, lasting through 1932. During 1929-32, 85,000 businesses failed; national income declined from $87.4 billions to $41.7 billions; agri-

cultural income was halved; the index of physical output
in manufacturing (1929 = 100) fell from 305 to 162;
total labor income declined 40 per cent. In March, 1933
(with the monthly average of 1923-25 as 100), the index of industrial production stood at 60; that of construction at 14; that of factory employment at 61; that
of factory payrolls at 38; that of wholesale prices at 60.
There were at least 15,000,000 unemployed. The burden
of debt, with the collapse in prices, had become intolerable.

Such were the problems facing the new administration
of Franklin D. Roosevelt in 1933. The revival of confidence in capitalist institutions stood first on the agenda.

— 9 —

THE NEW DEAL

Revolutions in American History.   There have been
three great turning points in the American economy and
these have notably occurred as a result of positive action
by government. The first stemmed from the adoption of
the Hamiltonian program (1791-95), the second from
that of the Republican party program (1861-65), and
the third from that of the New Deal (1933-39). In every
instance, responsibilities assumed by government toward
business—in directing, supporting, even subsidizing—
gave a new direction to enterprise and started it off on
hitherto unexplored paths.

The Hamiltonian program put its emphasis on finance:
the integrity of public and private credit would encourage accumulation and the investment functions in
America by both domestic and foreign risk-takers; at
the same time, it was willing to participate, as in the
federal government's purchase of a part of the stock

of the First Bank. The Republican program sought to
encourage industrialization and the expansion and diver-
sification of the domestic market: by high tariffs, large-
scale railroad construction, easy land and immigration
policies. It, too, was ready to participate, as in the case
of the subsidizing of many of the trunk railroads
through land grants and loans.

The New Deal as Revolution.   The New Deal went
further than its two predecessors: for not only did it
regulate and direct, but it also put government into
business. Following the adoption of the Hamiltonian
and Republican party programs, a great burst of new
energy and enterprise occurred, indeed, whole companies
of new innovators made their appearance. Fresh avenues
for investment were explored, opportunities for employment were opened up, new fortunes appeared: economic
change and economic progress went hand in hand. The
New Deal's contribution, perforce, was different. The
country was confronted by collapse; revival was the
prime necessity of the time; and every sort of expedient
—if not plan—was restorted to to put men back to work
and to start the wheels of industry revolving once more.

A new enterpriser now appeared, the government func-
tionary who headed a public corporation which could
buy and sell, lend and borrow, produce and distribute;
and this obviously was intervention of an entirely different order. In time, the directors of the New Deal referred to their activities as the "Welfare State": its purpose was as much to assure security as it was to promote
economic progress. And the chief method? It was that
of "deficit financing": government expenditures, by making possible the resumption of the normal industrial
processes, would encourage private enterprise to take up
the burden of advance. Only in part did this tactic suc-
ceed, for private companies were slow in following government's lead. Indeed, it was not until 1940—and in
the midst of war preparations—that the economy began
to leap ahead, increasing employment, capital formation,
real income.

Nevertheless, a revolution had occurred and it was
one that turned out to be permanent. It was this: government was assuming responsibility for the security and
welfare of its working populations and for the stability

of the whole economy. High employment, from thence on, was to be a concern of government; so was social security as regards old age and dependency; agriculture was to be protected against the mischances of the market; saving deposits were to be guaranteed. Even more profoundly, government accepted responsibility in these areas: it was to use its great weight to prevent too sharp swings in the business cycle (by monetary and fiscal controls, public-works planning and outlays); and it was to help in a more equitable distribution of the annual national product (by maintaining high real wages and by taxation). Here, in this last, the great lesson of the depression had been learned: the economy, associated with private enterprise, could endure and grow only if the purchasing power of its own producers was maintained at high levels. (*See Document No. 24.*)

New Deal Analysis of the Economy. The New Deal planners and managers operated upon certain theoretical assumptions: some were true, some false; some were maintained up to the end, and some were quickly abandoned.

1. It was assumed that, in many areas, capital plant had been overexpanded; it was imperative, in consequence, to limit new investment and production. This was true of agriculture, petroleum, and coal, and special authorities in each instance were set up to control production. The same idea was extended to all industry under the short-lived National Recovery Act of 1933-35, under which many industries, in the process of self-policing by the writing of "codes," were permitted to supervise the use of existing plant and new-plant expansion. John Maynard Keynes' ideas concerning limiting opportunities for investment (the existence already of a so-called "mature economy") were accepted by many New Deal economists; they looked, therefore, to social investment by government rather than to private investment by companies for the revival and rejuvenation of the economy.

2. Prices were being "managed," or they were "sticky" in important areas of enterprise, notably among the heavy-goods industries. This was due to imperfect competition; a frontal attack on monopoly practices was in order to reduce such rigidities.

3. Labor's position in the economy was an unequal one. Higher incomes would restore purchasing power; recognition of trade unions and collective bargaining would create checks on management vis-à-vis profits. Government also was to guarantee a minimum wage and maximum hours of work.

4. Debt burdens—notably onerous as prices continued to fall—had to be lightened. This was true of agriculture, municipalities, many industrial companies, privately owned homes.

5. The public-utilities industry was managed by holding companies on the one hand and was incapable of financing large-scale programs of new power installations on the other. Holding companies were to be dissolved; government was to help (particularly in rural areas) the financing of power transmission and the purchase of appliances; a great program of expansion in the Tennessee Valley was to be undertaken by a public corporation, the TVA.

6. Social security—against unemployment, old age, dependency—was a legitimate interest of government.

7. There were dark areas in cities and the countryside that required public concern: low-cost housing had to be built to help in the battle against the slums; marginal and submarginal farmers had to be helped; youth had to be put to work—on conservation projects if nothing else offered.

8. The whole banking system needed overhauling. Commercial banking had to be taken out of the investment banking business; the investor needed protection through supervision over houses issuing securities and the securities markets. Notably, central-banking needed strengthening to give government greater controls over the monetary and fiscal mechanisms.

9. The United States had to return to the world market on a sound footing. Freer trade had to be restored, at the same time that an orderly movement of American surpluses of cotton, cereals, tobacco, oil, and copper into foreign markets was devised. (*See Document No. 25.*)

Tactics of the New Deal. The programs of the New Deal planners, flowing from the above analysis, were pursued along the following lines:

1. Prices were to be restored and maintained. To

accomplish this, the dollar was devalued; gold and silver were purchased from abroad; limitations on the production of agricultural products, petroleum, and coal were imposed; industrial "codes of fair competition" (under the NIRA) were permitted to fix prices. In the case of agriculture, crop loans and subsidies were also required to make production control work.

2. Debt was to be reduced. The problem of debt was to be handled by price rise and by writing down debt. For agriculture, a public corporation, the Federal Farm Mortgage Corporation, made possible the exchange of privately held farm mortgages for semipublic (or public-guaranteed) mortgages. The Home Owners' Loan Corporation permitted the same kind of conversion in the case of residential mortgages. Bankruptcy laws were rewritten to give relief to businesses and municipalities.

4. Credit was to be revived and expanded. The Reconstruction Finance Corporation (created in 1932) was given large sums and vast powers to make loans to public bodies and private businesses. Virtual public control over the Federal Reserve System was established so that the expansion (and contraction) of credit would now be a concern of government. The Board of Governors of the Federal Reserve System now had the power to lower (and raise) the legal reserve requirements of banks and the right to raise (or lower) the margin requirements for the purchase of securities. As the New Deal resorted increasingly to deficit financing, with public securities flowing into banks, it was ready to accept the thought that the monetization of debt would take place and thus the way would be eased for the expansion of business credit.

5. Labor's purchasing power was to be raised. First in the codes written under the NIRA and then through the Fair Labor Standards Act of 1938, minimum wages and maximum hours were fixed and child labor was abolished. It was assumed that with the recognition of trade unions and the acceptance of collective bargaining, organized labor would be able to raise its own standards. The National (Wagner) Labor Relations Act of 1935 compelled bargaining with unions, once they had been established by election as the workers' representatives, but it also outlawed so-called unfair practices on the part of management.

6. Social security—against unemployment, invalidity, old age, dependency—was a responsibility of government. Many government agencies—Works Progress Administration, Public Works Administration, Civilian Conservation Corps—were set up to create jobs or induce public bodies, by loans, to embark on programs of public works. Unemployables were to be taken care of by local authorities, with financial assistance from the federal government. Funds were established to provide for the unemployed and the aged after retirement.

7. New homes were to be built with the help of federal subsidies.

8. The investor and saver were to be protected. The Securities and Exchange Commission was given wide authority over new corporate security issues and the activities of security exchanges. The Federal Deposit Insurance Corporation was set up to guarantee savings deposits in banks up to $5,000 (later raised to $10,000.)

9. The electric power and light industry was to be brought under closer public control. The Tennessee Valley Authority was created and with public funds it built a series of dams for the creation of power which in turn was to be sold to municipalities and farm cooperatives for transmission. Unnecessary holding companies in electric light and power were to be eliminated.

10. Foreign trade was to be revived. An Export-Import Bank was devised to finance the flow of goods and to extend credit to foreign governments if need be. Reciprocal trading agreements, written by the State Department, were to be used to effect the lowering of tariff barriers everywhere, largely through the employment of the device of most-favored-nation treatment.

Deficit Financing. Lending and spending were the chief resorts of the New Deal in creating employment and revitalizing the economy. This resulted in deficit financing, for debt was augmented to obtain the required funds. It loaned to distressed banks, railroads, insurance companies, mortgage corporations, and industrial concerns. It loaned to farmers, home owners, municipalities. It loaned—or authorized them to raise funds directly—to the newly established public authorities. It spent, by appropriation, subsidy, and grant-in-aid, to rehabilitate marginal farmers, to finance the building of ships, to put up low-cost housing, to construct public buildings, to provide flood control, roads, and reforestation, to launch writers, painters, and theater-arts projects. All this gave people work, added to the social assets of the nation—and increased the public debt. Debt did not trouble the New Deal planners as long as the national income was increased. But what if debt and fiscal policy generally (through taxation) did not revive private investment; then how permanent could such accomplishments really be? This was the question that began to be raised notably after 1938. (*See Document No. 26.*)

Position of Agriculture. On many fronts, the problems of agriculture were explored and remedies sought. To increase farmer purchasing power, the concept of "parity prices" (later, "parity income") was devised in an effort to bringing farm purchasing power back to the levels of 1909-14, when presumably agriculture was in balance with the rest of the economy. Farm production was to be adjusted to meet the needs of the market. Production was to be curtailed, and where surpluses appeared, they were to be held off the market by loans made to farmers. Also, soil conservation was to be pushed, mortgage debt was to be reduced, and efforts were to be made to rehabilitate marginal farmers.

The Agricultural Adjustment Act was passed in 1933 and continued on the statute books until 1936, when it was declared unconstitutional by the Supreme Court. Because overproduction was the difficulty, farmers were to receive "benefit payments" to encourage them to restrict plantings; funds for this purpose were to come from "processing taxes" on millers, cotton ginners, meat packers, and the like. It was this latter provision that the Supreme Court found illegal.

To continue controls and subsidies, the temporary Soil Conservation and Domestic Allotment Act and the Agricultural Adjustment Act of 1938 were passed. Both based government action on the necessity for protecting the land resources of the nation; subsidies—this time from government revenues—and loans were to continue. Both devices succeeded and agricultural prices—and the net income of farmers—began to rise. Net farm income stood at $6.1 billions in 1929, had fallen to $2 billions in 1932, and went up to $6 billions in 1937, dropping, however, to $4.5 billions in 1939. The parity ratio (percentage ratio of prices received by farmers to parity index) stood at 92 in 1929, had fallen to 58 in 1932, in 1937 stood at 93 and in 1939 at 77.

Position of Labor. The worker of the nation, to assure the establishment of collective-bargaining agencies and to create national minimums for wage and maximums for hours, received support from the National Labor Relations Act of 1935 and the Fair Labor Standards Act of 1938. The first required that employers bargain collectively with trade unions and surrender unfair labor practices; to enforce these requirements, a National Labor Relations Board was created which could decide which were the appropriate units for collective-bargaining purposes, conduct trade-union elections, and issue orders against the unfair conduct of management. The Fair Labor Standards Act established a 40-hour week (with time and a half for overtime), fixed 40 cents an hour as a minimum wage (raised to $1 an hour in 1956) and made possible the elimination of child labor by governmental order.

Trade unionism expanded under the AFL and the CIO (Committee, later Congress, for Industrial Organization). The latter, making its appearance in 1935, met with immediate successes in the unionization of the mass-production industries. The AFL also grew; in consequence, by 1941, each federation was claiming 4 million dues-paying members. The unions had direct impacts on salary increases and the adoption of fringe benefits (vacations with pay, retirement benefits, health insurance). It may very well be that during the 1930s, wages increased beyond productivity, reducing the marginal return of capital and therefore slowing down private investment. Thus, according to Professor Sumner H. Slichter, during 1921-26, physical productivity per manhour in manufacturing increased 4.3 per cent a year, while hourly earnings increased 8.4 per cent. On the other hand, during 1933-37, productivity per man hour went up only 1.7 per cent a year, while hourly earnings rose 40 per cent.

Course of Recovery. As a result of all these efforts on the part of government—but largely due to deficit financing—recovery was of a mixed character, production moving up from 1933 to 1937 but slipping back badly in that year. With 1947-49 as 100, the index of industrial production stood at 59 in 1929, 31 in 1932, 61 in 1937, and 48 in 1938. The figures for GNP [Gross National Product] (in billions of dollars, 1947 prices) were for the same years: 1929, $149.3 billions; 1932, $107.6 billions; 1937 $153.5 billions; 1938, $145.9 billions. On the other hand, the total labor force had increased from 49.4 millions in 1929 to 55 millions in 1938; in consequence, there continued to be sizable unemployment, possibly as much as 10 millions out of work. If recovery has been complete, and taking into consideration population increases and improvements in productivity during the decade (as much as 25 per cent), real GNP should have been fully 30 per cent higher.

Many factors contributed to the slowness of recovery. Higher labor costs, higher taxation, the mounting public debt bred no business confidence. There were charges being made that there was a "strike of capital," and this was probably so, because, despite all "easy money" efforts on the part of government, there was little significant increase in business loans.

The New Deal successes, as a result, were linked not so much with business expansion as with government spending. When deficit financing slowed down, as it did in 1937, recession at once set in, and only the resumption of public spending in 1938 and 1939 brought back revival.

Debt and Taxes.   Deficit financing was being pursued during the whole of the 1930s, and by the end of the decade the government debt had grown to more than $40 billions. This was largely due to an increase in expenditures. During 1931-35, federal expenditures were in the neighborhood of $4 billions annually; in 1934, they were $6 billions; and in 1937, $8.4 billions. For the years 1931-38, the total deficit was $20 billions.

Taxes mounted at the same time. Income taxes were pushed up, and in 1936, as a further tax on corporations, an undistributed-profits tax was levied. While this was abandoned in 1938, corporations nevertheless had little relief as far as losses were concerned. Federal taxes in 1931 came to $2.7 billions; in 1938, they were at $5.9 billions. The Revenue Acts, from 1932 to 1936, raised the maximum rate of the personal income tax from 25 to 79 per cent, the estate tax rate from a maximum of 20 to 70 per cent, imposed a new gifts tax with a maximum rate of 52 per cent, and increased the tax on capital gains. Arthur F. Burns, Chairman of the Council of Economic Advisers, commenting on this situation in 1956, pointed out: "These onerous taxes reduced the spending power of both individuals and businesses. Worse still, by coming in quick succession and creating uncertainty about the objectives of governmental policy, they weakened the incentives of businessmen and consumers to undertake capital expenditures. Innovation, private enterprise, and private investment languished."

All this was so. The other side of the shield was a willingness on the part of Americans to use the normal processes of discussion and action as they faced up to their difficulties. There was no widespread rejection of capitalist institutions as such. It was assumed, as a result of striving and experimentation, the American economy once more would begin its rise. This in fact, it did, from 1945 on. The Second World War intervened first.

— 10 —

HIGH PROSPERITY IN THE 1950s

The War's Impact. The United States entered World War II with the Japanese attack on Pearl Harbor (1941). An effort had been made to build up a conscript force before then, but, in 1941, the United States had only 1.5 million men under arms. The War's requirements, as it was waged all over the world, called for superhuman efforts; in consequence, some 770,000 officers for the army, 48,000 officers for the navy, and 15.1 million men were obtained for all the military establishments by draft.

The mobilization of industry was equally pervasive.
With the creation of the War Production Board in 1942,
fully 50 per cent of the nation's output was being de-
voted to war purposes. The WPB operated largely
through the establishment of priorities; and it was able
virtually to put an end to the manufacture of durable
consumers' goods as essential materials flowed into the
war effort. There were weaknesses in the systems of
controls, and the military and the WPB always did not
see eye to eye; yet, the war output reached extraordinary
levels. Some 12 million draftees actually under arms had
to be equipped in training camps and for combat; the
United States supplied $37 billions in Lend-Lease goods
(aid to the country's allies) of which $21 billions repre-
sented munitions and ships. Between 1939 and 1944,
manufacturing, mining, and construction doubled their
production (during World War I the increase was 7
per cent), while productive capacity went up by 50 per
cent. Over-all output increased by 25 per cent due to
a longer working week, improved equipment, and the
use of mass-production methods for aircraft manufacture and shipbuilding. The same tale was repeated in
the case of agriculture. With only 10 million workers
(against 11.47 million average of 1935-39) American
farms doubled their output during the war. Scarce machinery was utilized effectively; improved seeds and stock
strains and heavy employment of fertilizer played their
parts. Therefore, farm income doubled from 1939 to
1945 (as did also farm prices.)

Fiscal Problems. Almost all of this was accomplished by public expenditures: between 1941 and 1945,
public appropriations for war came to $347 billions. The
question of inflation was constantly uppermost in the
minds of administrators: both taxation and intensive
bonds sales were used to sop up additional purchasing
power and thus prevent a run on scarce consumer goods.
Between 1941 and 1945, the federal government obtained $97.35 billions in income and excess profits taxes
and $41.12 billions in excises, customs, and gift and
estate taxes. Eight war loans were floated, raising $156.9
billions, of which $43.3 billions were absorbed by in-
dividuals, the rest being taken up by banks largely. To
prevent a runaway inflation, due to increased payrolls

and the potential credit expansion of which the banks were capable on the one hand, and shortness of supply in consumer goods on the other, price controls were imperative. The Office of Price Administration was set up and it worked heroically with myriads of problems—freezing stocks of scarce goods and then rationing them to consumers, fixing prices, establishing ceilings for rents, and the like. In October, 1942, finally, OPA controls were extended to wages. To hold the activities of banks in leash, the Federal Reserve System raised the reserve requirements of banks, and set limits on installment credit. The country's interest-bearing debt mounted from $34.7 billions in 1939 to $256.4 billions in 1945. Price controls met with only measurable success, as one would expect. The all-commodity price index $(1926 = 100)$ rose from 77.1 in 1939 to 105.8 in 1945; the index of raw-materials prices rose from 70.2 to 116.8.

Reconversion. Profiting from the experiences of World War I, Washington began to think of the processes of reconversion as early as 1944. Not only did millions of men, at the war's end, have to be demobilized and gradually reintroduced into the life of peacetime; not only did provision have to be made for the disposal of great stocks of surplus goods and the renegotiation of contracts; virtually the whole machinery of production had to be put back on a normal basis. But what was normal? Would there be a great army of the unemployed? (Some economists predicted it would total 8 millions six months after hostilities were terminated.) And what were the responsibilities of government as regards the creation of jobs and the stimulation of industrial efforts—through tax reduction, public-works planning, for example? Would the end of the war see deflation, industrial unrest, the collapse of agriculture once more?

To the astonishment of the world (and the confusion of the government economists) not deflation but inflation threatened. There existed extraordinary shortages in housing and automobiles; but more important, consumers had built up great reserves of disposal funds as a result of savings and purchases of bonds and war stamps. This backed-up demand at home as well as the virtually limitless needs of all countries engaged in the war for reconstruction of bombed-out areas, replacement of obsolescent plants, and raw-material stocks, started off an unprecedented boom in America which continued (except for occasional mild recession) through the 1950s.

The elimination of wartime controls occurred swiftly. Wage controls went first as the result of a round of strikes in key industries between November, 1945, and January, 1946; "fact-finding" boards, established by the President, recommended wage increases averaging 15 cents an hour. Price controls were generally abandoned by midsummer, 1946, only the controls on rents remaining. All this, of course, to the accompaniment of inflation. The consumer price index (1947-49 = 100) went up from 59.9 in 1940 to 76.9 in 1945 and 102.8 in 1950. Despite the miracles of productivity and constant wage increases, real income per capita declined somewhat in the postwar period.

In constant (1955) dollars, the per capita disposable personal income, stood as follows for the indicated years: 1940, $1,101; 1945, $1,600; 1950, $1,513. It was not until 1955 that per capita income went above that of 1945; in 1955, it was $1,629. Here, in this single set of figures is revealed the impressive character of the American advances; for, in the 15 years 1940-55, the real income of every man, woman, and child in America, for spending and saving, increased 48 per cent!

Aspects of Prosperity. On every side there were evidences of the great well-being of Americans in the 1950s. Foreign aid (grants and loans came to $50 billions during 1945-51) played a part in stimulating the new prosperity; so did, too, the increase in government outlays once more to finance the Korean War (1950-53). But far more important were the greater productivity of American workers; the willingness of business to invest in new enterprise, new processes, and new machines; and the constantly mounting capacity to consume of the American public. Confidence had been restored in the capitalist processes. Government stood by—by monetary and fiscal controls, a willingness to finance long-term public improvements—to prevent sharp swings in the business cycle. Rather than hoarding by companies and, therefore, the existence of idle funds, business was spend-

ing billions each year on new capital creation. There
were safeguards built into the economy against serious
recessions in the savings of individuals, unemployment
and welfare funds, social security, and price-protection
for agriculture. At the same time, American direct investments overseas were beginning to mount, demon-
strating that by the arts of peace Americans were seeking to do their share in raising standards of production
and living among underdeveloped countries.

Political changes had little effects on fundamental
commitments. The Truman Administrations (1945-53)
and the Eisenhower Administration (1955-57) accepted
governmental concern over the well-being of the American people—as regards full employment, social security,
health, housing, education, and civil rights. Thus, President Eisenhower was prepared to take the government
out of the economy; but he advocated public assistance
for highway construction, slum clearance and housing,
education and health. He substituted flexible price controls for inflexible ones for agriculture; but the floors
under prices still were kept high. (*See Document No.
27.*)

The National Income and its Division. In terms
of 1955 prices the Gross National Product rose from
$207.4 billions in 1940 to $317.5 billions in 1945 and
$387.4 billions in 1955. In 1956, it was over $400 billions. How great a role private domestic investment was
playing in the economy will be noted from these figures
(also in 1955 dollars): 1940, $29.8 billions; 1945, $17.6
billions; 1955, $59.4 billions. The advances in per capita
disposable personal income have already been alluded
to. The same tale was to be found in the case of per
capita personal consumption expenditures. In 1955 dollars, these were as follows: 1940, $1,040; 1945, $1,295;
1955, $1,527.

Other Indexes. In the 1950s, every year, more
than 1 million new residential units were being constructed; in fact, 60 per cent of American families owned
their own homes. At least 70 million Americans had
money in savings accounts; 115 million owned life insurance; and 10 million owned shares in American companies. Farm assets reached an all-time record of $170.1
billions at the end of 1955, with 75 per cent of Ameri-

can farmers owning their own land. Mortgage debt was
only $9 billions in the same year. Realized net income
of farm operators in 1955 stood at $11.3 billions (as
compared with $12.86 billions in 1950 and $6.1 billions
in 1929). That is to say, while farm income lagged and,
therefore, agricultural real income did not keep pace
with other sectors of the economy, the position of
farmers as proprietors was better than it had been for
35 years. Total private foreign holdings of Americans
came to $29 billions at the end of 1955, an increase of
almost $2.5 billions over the previous year. In mid-
summer 1956, there were 66.8 million in the total civilian labor force, with less than 3 millions unemployed.
(*See Document No. 28.*)

Rigidities and Uncertainties. This did not mean
there were neither rigidities nor soft spots in the
economy, for there were. A new wave of mergers was
taking place in the 1950s, threatening the same inflexibility of prices that was a characteristic of the economy
of the 1920s. Consumer credit was beginning to mount
to alarming proportions. Labor, for its part, was obtaining contracts under which wages were being tied to the
cost-of-living index rather than to productivity. The
position of agriculture was not as favorable as it might
have been. While investments overseas were beginning
to mount, they were not nearly as large as they should
be if the United States was to assist underdeveloped
countries in their battle against poverty (and the bland-
ishments of communism). Nor were Americans completely assured that monetary and fiscal controls could
handle the inflation that was a constant problem because of wage increases and the pressure of consumers
for credit to build homes, buy automobiles, finance
travel, and the like. There continued to be large, un-
fulfilled wants: in the eradication of slums, the improvement of submarginal farms, the building of schools, the
meeting of medical costs. (*See Document No. 29.*)

American Capitalism in the 1950s. To say these
things was to say that capitalism—which depended upon
risks taken and decisions made by private enterprisers
and not by government—possessed instabilities. The business cycle with recurrent recession and runaway boom
had not been eliminated and probably could not ever

be entirely controlled. But advances had been made as a result of the acceptance of both governmental and business responsibilities. There was no doubt that the capitalist economy of America was resting on a firmer and broader base than ever before in its history: in the improved real income of its people, the mounting productivity of its industrial and farming plant, the savings of its population.

Socially, this gain was most impressive: the spread between income receivers was narrowing, so that while large incomes were not disappearing, poverty was being sharply decreased and the middle-income groups were constituting the great backbone of America. In 1935-36, more than 50 per cent of America's families had annual incomes less than $1000; in 1954, only 10 per cent. In 1935-36, less than 3 per cent of America's families had annual incomes over $5000; in 1954, the proportion was more than 30 per cent! It was no wonder that the American people—workers, farmers, proprietors, managers—accepted capitalism, with its processes of private accumulation and investment and its unequal wealth and income, as their habitual way of life. There was no radicalism in America. The tiny Communist party did not speak for the workers, but for a small group of individuals unhesitatingly following the Soviet Union. There was no Socialist party and the syndicalist movement was dead. Trade unionism, although widening its horizons somewhat since the AFL of Samuel Gompers, still accepted the industrial leadership of private enterprise. (*See Document No. 30.*)

The Responsibilities of Capitalism. The capitalism of the 1950s had moved far from its beginnings under the general merchants of the colonial and national periods, and the owners-managers of the post-Civil War era. While small business continued to exist and large numbers of new ventures appeared every year, the corporation as the unit of organization had become the rule. In heavy industry, transportation, and banking, consolidations were reducing the number of concerns and the competitive units. This did not mean that incentives were diminishing. For the same impulses that guided the conduct of the early American capitalists—desire for social recognition, the need for accomplishment, prestige, provision for one's family—were spurring on the executives managing American big business. They worked as hard; they thought as much of profits and productivity; they were just as competitive with one another for recognition and with other industries, with the accents on quality if not on price.

Indeed, the new managers had moved ahead of the earlier innovators in these particulars. They recognized that the soundness of the economy, while still linked with profits, was founded on an ever-growing distribution which could be successful only if real income continued to move up. The welfare of the whole American people spelled the success or failure of American capitalism. In the second place, in a democratic society, the managers constantly had to justify their policies before stockholders, the trade unions, and the legislative bodies of the federal and state governments. To this extent— and unlike the tactics of authoritarian and totalitarian societies—American capitalism operated in the open, sustaining itself by its accomplishment and its promise.

For equality of opportunity—the ability of men of talents to rise, in large part as a result of the constant expansion of the educational system—continued to exist. As long as it did so and as long as redistribution of wealth and income took place, capitalism would be the accepted credo of the American people.

The Challenges of Capitalism. The challenges to American capitalism did not come from within; they came from without—from Soviet Russia and its satellites, from communist China, from the squalor and poverty of Africa and the Near and Middle East. Communism promised security (coupled with totalitarian rule and the extinction of freedom). The struggling new states, raising the banner of release from colonialism, could hold popular support only by promising glittering reforms for which they possessed neither the wealth nor the individual skills. Regeneration was possible, of course; but it required toil, patience, and public integrity —to discharge international obligations, protect the investments of foreigners, maintain regimes founded securely on law.

In the final analysis, American capitalism would survive only if—by its example, influence, and help—it could extend the boundaries of freedom and once more assist in the re-establishment of an international community where the mobility of goods, labor, and capital existed. This was the agenda for the future and the promise—or extinction—of American capitalism. Within its own sphere, it had demonstrated amply that human welfare, in a climate of individual freedom, is realizable by the processes of private accumulation and investment where business decision-making is a function of individuals and not of state authority.

Part II

DOCUMENTS

— Document No. 1 —

THE ENGLAND FROM WHICH THE SETTLERS CAME[1]

The England from which most of the American settlers came was an unequal society where opportunities for the little men were few because of class restrictions, monopoly privileges, and a general hostility to the working classes. The two selections presented below exemplify this state of affairs. William Harrison was a contemporary of Shakespeare. Sir John Colepeper was one of the members of Parliament who denounced the absolutism of the English monarchy and called attention to the misdeeds of the monopolies; his speech was delivered during the great debate of 16 Charles I, 1640.

❦   ❦   ❦

I

The fourth and last sort of people in England are daie labourers, poore husbandmen, and some retailers (which haue no frée land) copie holders, and all artificers, as tailers, shomakers, carpenters, brickmakers, masons, &c. As for slaues and bondmen we haue none, naie such is the priuilege of our countrie by the especiall grace of God, and bountie of our princes, that if anie come hither from other realms, so soone as they set foot on land they become so frée of condition as their master, whereby all note of seruile bondage is vtterlie remooued from them, wherein we resemble (not the

[1] The first selection is from William Harrison's "An Historical Description of the Island of Britain. . . ." in Holinshed's *Chronicles* (London, 1586). The second is reprinted from William Cobbett, ed., *Parliamentary History of England,* Vol. II (London, 1807).

Germans who had slaues also, though such as in respect
of the slaues of other countries might well be reputed
frée, but) the old Indians and the Taprobanes, who
supposed it a great iniurie to nature to make or suffer
them to be bond whome she in hir woonted course
dooth product and bring foorth frée. This fourth and
last sort of people therefore haue neither voice nor authorities in the common wealth, but are to be ruled,
and not to rule other: yet they are no altogither neglected, for in cities and corporate townes, for default of
yeomen they are faine to make up their inquests of such
maner of people. And in villages they are commonlie
made churchwardens, sidemen, aleconners, now and then
constables, and manie times inioie the name of hedbor-
oughes. Vnto this sort also may our great swarmes of
idle seruing men be referred, of whome there runneth
a prouerbe; Yoong seruing men old beggers, bicause
seruice is none heritage. These men are profitable to
none, for if their condition be well perused, they are
enimies to their masters, to their freends, and to them-
selues: for by them oftentimes their masters are in-
couraged vnto vnlawfull exactions of their tenants, their
fréends brought vnto pouertie by their rents inhanced,
and they themselves brought to confusion by their owne
prodigalitie and errors, as men that hauing not where-
with of their owne to mainteine their excesses, doo search
in high waies, budgets, cofers, males, and stables, which
way to supplie their wants. . . .

II

I have but one Grievance more to offer unto you;
but this one compriseth many: it is a nest of wasps, or
swarm of vermin, which have over-crept the land. I
mean the monopolers and polers of the people: These
like the frogs of Egypt, have got possession of our
dwellings, and we have scarce a room free from them:
they sip in our cup, they slip in our dish, they sit by
our fire; we find them in the dye-vat, wash-bowl, and
powdering-tub; they share with the butler in his box,
they have marked and scaled us from head to foot. Mr.
Speaker, they will not bate us a pin: we may not buy
our own cloaths without their brokage. These are the
leeches that have sucked the commonwealth so hard,

that it is almost become hectical. And, some of these
are ashamed of their right names; they have a vizard
to hide the brand made by that good law in the last
parliament of king James; they shelter themselves under
the name of a corporation; they make bye-laws, which
serve their turns to squeeze us, and fill their purses:
unface these, and they will prove us bad cards as any
in the pack. These are not petty chapmen, but wholesale men. Mr. Speaker, I have echoed to you the cries
of the kingdom; . . .

— Document No. 2 —

THE MERCANTILIST SYSTEM [2]

*America had friends in Britain, among them Edmund
Burke and Adam Smith. It was Smith who systematically
sought to undermine the whole program of protection
associated with the mercantilist system. Again and again,
he reverted to the controls Britain had imposed on the
colonial economic life. In a characteristic passage he
attacked British policy: "To prohibit a great people from
making all that they can of every part of their own
produce, or from employing their stock [capital] and
their industry in the way that they judge most advantageous to themselves, is a manifest violation of the most
sacred rights of mankind."*

To found a great empire for the sole purpose of raising up a people of customers, may at first sight appear a
project fit only for a nation of shopkeepers. It is, however, a project altogether unfit for a nation of shop-

[2] Adam Smith, *The Wealth of Nations* (London, 1776), Bk.
IV, ch. vii, part III.

keepers, but extremely fit for a nation whose government is influenced by shopkeepers. Such statesmen, and such statesmen only, are capable of fancying that they will find some advantage in employing the blood and treasure of their fellow-citizens, to found and maintain such an empire. Say to a shopkeeper, Buy me a good estate, and I shall always buy my clothes at your shop, even though I should pay somewhat dearer than what I can have them for at other shops; and you will not find him very forward to embrace your proposal. But should any other person buy you such an estate, the shopkeeper will be much obliged to your benefactor if he would enjoin you to buy all your clothes at his shop. England purchased from some of her subjects, who found themselves uneasy at home, a great estate in a distant country. The price, indeed, was very small, and instead of thirty years' purchase, the ordinary price of land in the present times, it amounted to little more than the expense of the different equipments which made the first discovery, reconnoitred the coast, and took a fictitious possession of the country. The land was good and of great extent, and the cultivators having plenty of good ground to work upon, and being for some time at liberty to sell their produce where they pleased, became in the course of little more than thirty or forty years (between 1620 and 1660) so numerous and thriving a people, that the shopkeepers and other traders of England wished to secure to themselves the monopoly of their custom. Without pretending, therefore, that they had paid any part, either of the original purchase-money, or of the subsequent expense of improvement, they petitioned the parliament that the cultivators of America might for the fuure be confined to their shop; first, for buying all the goods which they wanted from Europe; and, secondly, for selling all such parts of their own produce as those traders might find it convenient to buy. For they did not find it convenient to buy every part of it. Some parts of it imported into England might have interfered with some of the trades which they themselves carried on at home. Those particular parts of it, therefore, they were willing that the colonists should sell where they could; the farther off the better; and upon that account proposed that their market should be confined to the coun

tries south of Cape Finisterre. A clause in the famous act
of navigation established this truly shopkeeper proposal
into a law.

The maintenance of this monopoly has hitherto been
the principal, or more properly perhaps the sole end and
purpose of the dominion which Great Britain assumes
over her colonies. . . .

Under the present system of management, therefore,
Great Britain derives nothing but loss from the dominion
which she assumes over her colonies.

To propose that Great Britain should voluntarily give
up all authority over her colonies, and leave them to
elect their own magistrates, to enact their own laws, and
to make peace and war as they might think proper, would
be to propose such a measure as never was, and never
will be adopted by any nation in the world. No nation
ever voluntarily gave up the dominion of any provence,
how troublesome soever it might be to govern it, and
how small soever the revenue which it afforded might be
in proportion to the expence which it occasioned. Such
sacrifices, though they might frequently be agreeable to
the interest, are always mortifying to the pride of every
nation, and, what is perhaps of still greater consequence,
they are always contrary to the private interest of the
governing part of it, who would thereby be deprived of
the disposal of many places of trust and profit, of many
opportunities of acquiring wealth and distinction, which
the possession of the most turbulent, and, to the great
body of the people the most unprofitable province seldom
fails to afford. The most visionary enthusiasts would
scarce be capable of proposing such a measure, with any
serious hopes at least of its ever being adopted. If it was
adopted, however, Great Britain would not only be
immediately freed from the whole annual expence of the
peace establishment of the colonies, but might settle
with them such a treaty of commerce as would effectually
secure to her a free trade, more advantageous to the
great body of the people, though less so to the merchants,
than the monopoly which she at present enjoys. By thus
parting good friends, the natural affection of the colonies
to the mother country which, perhaps, our late dissen-
sions have well nigh extinguished, would quickly revive.
It might dispose them not only to respect, for whole cen-

turies together, that treaty of commerce which they had concluded with us at parting, but to favour us in war as well as in trade, and, instead of turbulent and factious subjects, to become our most faithful, affectionate, and generous allies; and the same sort of parental affection on the one side, and filial respect on the other, might revive between Great Britain and her colonies, which used to subsist between those of ancient Greece and the mother city from which they descended.

— Document No. 3 —

THE LORDS COMMISSIONERS OF TRADE AND PLANTATIONS TO THE HOUSE OF COMMONS [3]

English officialdom watched carefully the economic development of the colonies not only to prevent rivalry with the mother country but to encourage those activities which could improve the English balance of trade. Here is a characteristic statement prepared during 1731-32.

✓   ✓   ✓

Pursuant to an order of the British house of commons, directed to the lords commissioners of trade and plantations in the later end of the last, or the beginning of this (1732) year, relating to the dispute still subsisting between the sugar colonies, and the nothern continental colonies of America, that board reported, with respect to laws made, manufactures set up, or trade carried on, there, detrimental to the trade, navigation, or manufactures, of Great Britain, as follows, viz. . . .

By later accounts from Massachusetts-bay in New-

[3] David Macpherson, *Annals of Commerce* (4 vols., London, 1805), vol. III, pp. 186-91.

England, the assembly have voted a bounty of 30s. for every piece of duck or canvas made in the province. Some other manufactures are carried on there, as brown Hollands for women's wear, which lessens the importation of calicoes, and some other sorts of East-India goods. They also make some small quantities of cloth, made of linen and cotton, for ordinary shirting and sheeting. By a papermill set up three years ago, they make to the value of £200 sterling yearly. There are also several forges for making bar iron, and some furnaces for cast iron, or hollow ware, and one slittling mill, and a manufacture of nails.

The governor writes concerning the woollen manufacture, that the country people, who used formerly to make most of their clothing out of their own wool, do not now make a third part of what they wear, but are mostly clothed with British manufactures. The same governor (Belcher) by some of his letters of an older date, in answer to our annual queries, writes, that there are some few copper mines in this province, but so far distant from water-carriage, and the ore so poor, that it is not worth the digging. The surveyor-general of his majesty's woods writes, that they have in New-England six furnaces and nineteen forges for making iron; and that in this province many ships are built for the French and Spaniards, in return for rum, molasses, wines, and silks, which they truck there, by connivance. Great quantities of hats are made in New-England, of which the company of hatters of London have likewise lately complained to us. That great quantities of those hats are exported to Spain, Portugal, and our West-India islands. They also make all sorts of iron work for shipping. There are several still-houses and sugar-bakers established in New-England.

From the foregoing state, it is observable, that there are more trades carried on, and manufactures set up, in the provinces on the continent of America to the northward of Virginia, prejudicial to the trade and manufactures of Great Britain, particularly in New-England, than in any other of the British colonies; which is not to be wondered at: for their soil, climate, and produce, being pretty near the same with ours, they have no staple commodities of their own growth to exchange for our manufactures;

which puts them under greater necessity, as well as under greater temptation, of providing for themselves at home; to which may be added, in the charter governments, the little dependence they have upon the mother country, and consequently the small restraints, they are under in any matters detrimental to her interests.

And therefor, we would humbly beg leave to report and submit to the wisdom of this honourable house, the substance of what we formerly proposed in our report on the silk, linen, and woollen, manufactures herein before recited; namely, whether it might not be expedient to give those colonies proper encouragements for turning their industry to such manufactures and products as might be of service to Great Britain, and more particularly to the production of all kinds of naval stores.— (Signed) Paul Dockminique &c. Whitehall, February 15, 1731-2.

— Document No. 4 —

COLONIAL CURRENCY TROUBLES [4]

The constant pinch in the colonies for currency and credit led to all sorts of devices for expanding the money supply. The preoccupation with money in America has a long history, as this selection shows, for Thomas Pownall was governor of the Massachusetts Bay Colony in the 1760's.

The British American colonies have not, within themselves, the means of making money or coin. They cannot acquire it from Great Britain, the balance of trade being

[4] Thomas Pownall, *The Administration of the Colonies* (London, 1764), pp. 102-13.

against them. The returns of those branches of commerce, in which they are permitted to trade to any other part of Europe, are but barely sufficient to pay this balance. By the present act of navigation, they are prohibited from trading with the colonies of any other nations, so that there remains nothing but a small branch of African trade, and the scrambling profits of an undescribed traffic, to supply them with silver. However, the fact is, and matters have been so managed, that the general currency of the colonies used to be in Spanish and Portuguese coin. This supplied the internal circulation of their home business, and always finally came to England in payments for what the colonists exported from thence. If the act of navigation should be carried into such rigorous execution as to cut off this supply of a silver currency to the colonies, the thoughts of administration should be turned to the devising some means of supplying the colonies with money of some sort of other. . . .

The safest and wisest measure which government can take, is not to discourage or obstruct that channel through which silver flows into the colonies, nor to interfere with that value which it acquires there; but only so to regulate the colony trade, that silver shall finally come to, and center in Great Britain, whither it will most certainly come in its true value; but if through any fatality in things or measures, a medium of trade, a currency of money, should grow defective in the colonies, the wisdom of government will then interpose, either to remedy the cause which occasions such defect, or to contrive the means of supplying the deficiency. The remedy lies in a certain address in carrying into execution the act of navigation; but if that remedy is neglected, the next recourse must lie in some means of maintaining a currency specially appropriated to the colonies, and must be partly such as will keep a certain quantity of silver coin in circulation there,—and partly such as shall establish *a paper currency,* holding a value nearly equal to silver. . . .

An encreasing country of settlers and traders must always have the balance of trade against them, for this very reason, because they are encreasing and improving, because they must be continually wanting further supplies which their present circumstances will neither furnish nor pay for:—And for this very reason also, they must alway labour under a decreasing silver currency, though their circumstances require an encreasing one. In the common cursory view of things, our politicians, both theorists and practitioners, are apt to think, that a country which has the balance of trade against it, and is continually drained of its silver currency, must be in a declining state; but here we may see that the progressive improvements of a commercial country of settlers, must necessarily have the balance of trade against them, and a decreasing silver currency; that their continual want of money and other materials to carry on their trade and business must engage them in debt—But that those very things applied to their improvements, will in return not only pay those debts, but create also a surplus to be still carried forward to further and further improvements. In a country under such circumstances, money lent upon interest to settlers, creates money. Paper money thus lent upon interest will create gold and silver in principal, *while the interest becomes a revenue that pays the charges of government*. This currency is the true Pactolian stream which converts all into gold that is washed by it. It is on this principal that the wisdom and virtue of the assembly of Pennsylvania established, under the sanction of government, an office for the emission of paper money by loan. . . . This paper money consists of promissory notes, issued by the authority of the legislature of each province, deriving its value from being payable at a certain period, by monies arising from a tax proportioned to that payment at the time fixed. These notes pass as lawful money, and have been hitherto a legal tender in each respective province where they are issued.

— Document No. 5 —

REMONSTRANCE OF THE COLONY OF RHODE ISLAND TO THE LORDS COMMISSIONERS OF TRADE AND PLANTATIONS[5]

The old British Empire, in furthering its mercantilist policies, found itself in difficulties after the war with France was over in 1763. To raise revenues and to protect its possessions in the West Indies, Parliament began to discriminate against the northern colonies. In 1764 Rhode Island protested; this statement is an excellent demonstration of the weaknesses of the mercantilist system.

✓   ✓   ✓

To the Right Honorable the Lords Commissioners for Trade and Plantations; humbly show:

The Governor and Company of the English colony of Rhode Island and Providence Plantations, in New England, in America, convened at South Kingstown, the 24th day of January, A.D., 1764, in behalf of themselves and their constituents, the merchants, planters and traders in said colony—

That the act passed in the sixth year of the reign of His late Majesty George II., commonly called the sugar act, being to expire at the end of the present session Parliament; and as the same, if continued, may be highly injurious and detrimental to all His Majesty's North American colonies in general, and to this colony in particular, the said Governor and Company presume to offer some considerations drawn from the particular state and

[5] *Records of the Colony of Rhode Island and Providence Plantations, in New England,* VI, pp. 378-83.

circumstances of said colony, against the renewal of said act. . . .

In doing this, it is hoped that the interest and advantage of the mother country, will be found to coincide with that of the colony, in the extinction of a law, conceived to be prejudicial to both.

The colony of Rhode Island included not a much larger extent of territory than about thirty miles square; and of this, a great part is a barren soil, not worth the expense of cultivation; the number of souls in it, amount to forty-eight thousand, of which the two seaport towns of Newport and Providence, contain near one-third. The colony hath no staple commodity for exportation, and does not raise provisions sufficient for its own consumption; yet, the goodness of its harbors, and its convenient situation for trade, agreeing with the spirit and industry of the people, hath in some measure supplied the deficiency of its natural produce, and provided the means of subsistence to its inhabitants.

By a moderate calculation, the quantity of British manufactures and other goods of every kind imported from Great Britain, and annually consumed in this colony, amount at least to £120,000, sterling, part of which is imported directly into the colony; but as remittances are more easily made to the neighbouring province of the Massachusetts Bay, Pennsylvania and New York, than to Great Britain, a considerable part is purchased from them.

This sum of £120,000, sterling, may be considered as a debt due from the colony, the payment of which is the great object of every branch of commerce, carried on by its inhabitants, and exercises the skill and invention of every trader. . . .

As there is no commodity raised in the colony suitable for the European market, but the few articles aforementioned; and as the other goods raised for exportation, will answer at no market but in the West Indies, it necessarily follows that the trade thither must be the foundation of all our commerce; and it is undoubtedly true, that solely from the prosecution of this trade with the other branches that are pursued in consequence of it, arises the ability to pay for such quantities of British goods.

It appears from the custom house books, in Newport,

that from January, 1763, to January, 1764, there were one hundred and eighty-four sail of vessels bound on foreign voyages. . . .

Of these foreign vessels, about one hundred and fifty are annually employed in the West India trade, which import into this colony about fourteen thousand hogsheads of molasses; whereof, a quantity, not exceeding twenty-five hundred hogsheads, come from all the English islands together.

It is this quantity of molasses which serves as an engine in the hands of the merchant to effect the great purpose of paying for British manufactures; for part of it is exported to the Massachusetts Bay, to New York and Pennsylvania, to pay for British goods, for provisions and for many articles which compose our West India cargoes; and part to the other colonies, southward of these last mentioned, for such commodities as serve for a remittance immediately to Europe; such as rice, naval stores, &c., or such as are necessary to enable us to carry on our commerce; the remainder (besides what is consumed by the inhabitants) is distilled into rum, and exported to the coast of Africa; nor will this trade to Africa appear to be of little consequence, if the following account of it be considered.

From this deduction of the course of our trade, which is founded in exact truth, it appears that the whole trading stock of this colony, in its beginning, progress and end is uniformly directed to the payment of the debt contracted by the importation of British goods; and it also clearly appears, that without this trade, it would have been and always will be, utterly impossible for the inhabitants of this colony to subsist themselves, or to pay for any considerable quantity of British goods. . . .

— Document No. 6 —

THE CRITICAL PERIOD⁶

Madison and Hamilton notably among the Founding Fathers were quick to see the inadequacies of the Confederation. Not only was the Congress incapable of providing a revenue and maintaining the public credit, but the states were resorting to all sorts of dubious devices to cope with business decline. James Madison was keeping Jefferson—away in France as the American minister— informed of domestic affairs; the selection below was a letter written in 1785.

✓   ✓   ✓

Unhappily there are but too many belonging to the opposite side of the acc^t. At the head of these is to be put the general rage for paper money. Pen^a. & N. Carolina took the lead in this folly. In the former the sum emitted was not considerable, the funds for sinking it were good, and it was not made a legal tender. It issued into circulation partly by way of loan to individuals on landed security, partly by way of payment to the public creditors. Its present depreciation is about 10 or 12 per c^t. In N. Carolina the sums issued at different times has been of greater amount, and it has constantly been a tender. It issued partly in payments to military creditors and latterly, in purchases of Tob^o. on public account. The Agent I am informed was authorised to give nearly the double of the current price, and as the paper was a tender, debtors ran to him with their Tob^o., and the creditors paid the expence of the farce. The depreciation is said to be 25 or 30 per c^t. in that State. S. Carolina was the next in order. Her emission was in the way of loans to individuals, and is not a legal tender. But land

⁶ James Madison, *Writings,* Gaillard Hunt, ed., 9 vols. (New York 1900-10), vol. II.

is there made a tender in case of suits which shuts the
Courts of Justice, and is perhaps as great an evil. The
friends of the emission say that it has not yet depreciated,
but they admit that the price of commodities has risen,
which is evidently the form in which depreciation will
first shew itself. New Jersey has just issued £30,000
(dollars at 7s 6) in loans to her citizens. It is a legal
tender. An addition of £100,000 is shortly to follow on
the same principles. The terror of popular associations
stifles as yet an overt discrimination between it & specie;
but as this does not operate in Philad[a] & N. York where
all the trade of N.J. is carried on, its depreciation has
already commenced in those places & must soon com-
municate itself to N.J. New York is striking £200,000
(doll[r] at 8s.) on the plan of loans to her citizens. It is
made a legal tender in case of suits only. As it is but just
issuing from the press, its depreciation exists only in the
foresight of those who reason without prejudice on the
subject. In Rhode Island, £100,000 (dol[r] at 6s.) has
lately been issued in loans to individuals. It is not only
made a tender, but severe penalties annexed to the least
attempt direct or indirect to give a preference to specie.
Precautions dictated by distrust in the rulers soon produced it in the people. Supplies were withheld from the
Market, and the Shops were shut, popular meetings en-
sued, and the State remains in a sort of convulsion. . . .
  Whether Virg[a] is to remain exempt from the epidemic
malady will depend on the insuing Assembly. My hopes
rest chiefly on the exertions of Col. Mason and the failure of the experiments elsewhere. That these must fail
is morally certain; for besides the proofs of it already
visible in some States, and the intrinsic defect of the
paper in all, this fictitious money will rather feed than
cure the spirit of extravagance which sends away the coin
to pay the unfavorable balance, and will therefore soon
be carried to market to buy up coin for that purpose.
From that moment depreciation is inevitable. The value
of money consists in the uses it will serve. Specie will
serve all the uses of paper, paper will not serve one of
the essential uses of specie. The paper therefore will be
less valuable than specie. Among the numerous ills with
which this practice is pregnant, one I find is that it is
producing the same warfare & retaliation among the

States as were produced by the State regulations of commerce. Mass^ts & Connecticut have passed laws enabling their Citizens who are debtors to Citizens of States having their paper money, to pay their debts in the same manner as their Citizens who are creditors to Citizens of the latter States are liable to be paid their debts. . . .

— Document No. 7 —

THE FISCAL RESPONSIBILITIES OF GOVERNMENT[7]

Alexander Hamilton, as Secretary of the Treasury, had proposed the establishment of a bank, chartered by the federal government, which would both engage in a private banking business and act as the fiscal agent of the government. In fact, he foresaw the need for central banking and the role of the bank in such a relationship. He was given the opportunity to discuss at length the fiscal responsibilities of the government when Washington asked for opinions from him, Jefferson, and Randolph on the constitutionality of the bank. Hamilton replied February 23, 1791 in one of America's great state papers. It was here that he expounded the theory of "implied powers" of the constitution.

1   1   1

The proposed bank is to consist of an association of persons for the purpose of creating a joint capital to be employed, chiefly and essentially, in loans. So far the object is not only lawful, but is in the mere exercise of a right which the law allows to every individual. The

[7] *The Works of Alexander Hamilton,* J. C. Hamilton, ed., 7 vols. (New York 1850-51), vol. VII.

bank of New-York, which is not incorporated, is an example of such an association. The bill proposes, in addition, that the government shall become a joint proprietor in this undertaking; and that it shall permit the bills of the company, payable on demand, to be receivable in its revenues; and stipulates that it shall not grant privileges, similar to those which are to be allowed to this company, to any others. All this is incontrovertibly within the compass of the discretion of the government. The only question is, whether it has a right to incorporate this company, in order to enable it the more effectually to accomplish ends, which are in themselves lawful.

To establish such a right, it remains to show the relation of such an institution, to one or more of the specified powers of the government.

Accordingly, it is affirmed, that it has a relation, more or less direct, to the power of collecting taxes; to that of borrowing money; to that of regulating trade between the states; and to those of raising and maintaining fleets and armies. To the two former, the relation may be said to be immediate.

And, in the last place, it will be argued, that it is clearly within the provision, which authorizes the making of all *needful rules* and *regulations* concerning the property of the United States, as the same has been practised upon by the government.

A bank relates to the collection of taxes in two ways. *Indirectly,* by increasing the quantity of circulating medium, and quickening circulation, which facilitates the means of paying; *directly,* by creating a *convenient species* of medium in which they are to be paid.

To designate or appoint the money or thing in which taxes are to be paid, is not only a proper, but a necessary, *exercise* of the power of collecting them. Accordingly, Congress, in the law concerning the collection of the duties on imposts and tonnage, have provided that they shall be payable in gold and silver. But while it was an indispensable part of the work to say in what they should be paid, the choice of the specific thing was mere matter of discretion. The payment might have been required in the commodities themselves. Taxes in kind, however ill judged, are not without precedents even in the United States; or it might have been in the paper money of the several states, or in the bills of the bank of North-America, New-York, and Massachusetts, all or either of them; or it might have been in bills issued under the authority of the United States.

No part of this can, it is presumed, be disputed. The appointment, then, of the money or *thing* in which the taxes are to be paid, is an incident to the power of collection. And among the expedients which may be adopted, is that of bills issued under the authority of the United States.

Now the manner of issuing these bills, is again matter of discretion. The government might, doubtless, proceed in the following manner: It might provide that they should be issued under the direction of certain officers, payable on demand; and in order to support their credit, and give them a ready circulation, it might, besides giving them a currency in its taxes, set apart, out of any monies in its treasury a given sum, and appropriate it, under the direction of those officers, as a fund for answering the bills, as presented for payment.

The constitutionality of all this would not admit of a question, and yet it would amount to the institution of a bank, with a view to the more convenient collection of taxes. For the simplest and most precise idea of a bank, is, a deposit of coin or other property, as a fund for *circulating a credit* upon it, which is to answer the purpose of money. That such an arrangement would be equivalent to the establishment of a bank, would become obvious, if the place where the fund to be set apart was kept, should be made a receptacle of the monies of all other persons who should incline to deposit them there for safe keeping; and would become still more so, if the officers, charged with the direction of the fund, were authorized to make discounts at the usual rate of interest, upon good security. To deny the power of the government to add this ingredient to the plan, would be to refine away all government. . . .

— Document No. 8 —

REPORT ON MANUFACTURES[8]

In December, 1791, Alexander Hamilton submitted his great "Report on Manufactures" to Congress in which he asked for government support for manufacturing largely because of the unfavorable position the United States found itself in vis-à-vis the more advanced nations. Hamilton was arguing not from principle but from necessity; in fact, he was a libertarian in the Adam Smith sense. The whole report is imbued with the Smithian spirit; yet, curiously enough, it became the textbook of advocates of protective tariffs the world over. The selection below gives the Smithian argument for a "system of perfect liberty" and then advances the "infant industry" contention for government support.

✓   ✓   ✓

If the system of perfect liberty to industry and commerce were the prevailing system of nations, the arguments which dissuade a country, in the predicament of the United States, from the zealous pursuit of manufactures, would doubtless have great force. . . .

. . . But the system which has been mentioned is far from characterizing the general policy of nations. The prevalent one has been regulated by an opposite spirit. The consequence of it is, that the United States, are, to a certain extent, in the situation of a country precluded from foreign commerce. They can, indeed, without difficulty, obtain from abroad the manufactured supplies of which they are in want; but they experience numerous and very injurious impediments to the emission and vent of their own commodities. Nor is this the case in reference to a single foreign nation only. The regulations of several countries, with which we have the

[8] Reprinted from the *Works of Alexander Hamilton*, J. C. Hamilton, ed., 7 vols. (New York 1850-51), vol. VII.

most extensive intercourse, throw serious obstructions in the way of the principal staples of the United States.

In such a position of things, the United States cannot exchange with Europe on equal terms; and the want of reciprocity would render them the victim of a system which should induce them to confine their views to agriculture, and refrain from manufactures. A constant and increasing inecessity, on their part, for the commodities of Europe, and only a partial and occasional demand for their own, in return, could not but expose them to a state of impoverishment, compared with the opulence to which their political and natural advantages authorize them to aspire. . . .

The remaining objections to a particular encouragement of manufactures in the United States now require to be examined.

One of these turns on the proposition, that industry, if left to itself, will naturally find its way to the most useful and profitable employment. Whence it is inferred that manufactures, without the aid of government, will grow up as soon and as fast as the natural state of things and the interest of the community may require.

Against the solidity of this hypothesis, in the full latitude of the terms, very cogent reasons may be offered. These have relation to the strong influence of habit and the spirit of imitation; the fear of want of success in untried enterprises; the intrinsic difficulties incident to first essays towards a competition with those who have previously attained to perfection in the business to be attempted: the bounties, premiums, and other artificial encouragements with which foreign nations second the exertions of their own citizens, in the branches in which they are to be rivalled.

Experience teaches, that men are often so much governed by what they are accustomed to see and practise, that the simplest and most obvious improvements, in the most ordinary occupations, are adopted with hesitation, reluctance, and by slow gradations. The spontaneous transition to new pursuits, in a community long habituated to different ones, may be expected to be attended with proportionably greater difficulty. When former occupations ceased to yield a profit adequate to the subsistence of their followers, or when there was an absolute

deficiency of employment in them, owing to the super-
abundance of hands, changes would ensue; but these
changes would be likely to be more tardy than might
consist with the interest either of individuals or of the
society. . . .

— Document No. 9 —

LAND OF OPPORTUNITY[9]

*Americans knew, from the beginning, that opportun-
ities for the humblest presented themselves in the new
continent. As early as 1751 Benjamin Franklin had
called attention to the facts that cheap lands and high
wages permitted America to stand apart from the rest of
the world. J. Hector St. John de Crèvecoeur repeated the
tale, in more idyllic form, in his* Letters from an American Farmer. *He caught another note as well, that of an
American nationalism, which the common experiences
in the Revolution had helped to fuse. Crèvecoeur first
came to America in the 1760's and stayed for two decades. He returned to Europe ultimately; but it is apparent
where his loyalties really were. The* Letters *appeared in
London in 1782.*

✓   ✓   ✓

I wish I could be acquainted with the feelings and
thoughts which must agitate the heart and present themselves to the mind of an enlightened Englishman, when
he first lands on this continent. He must greatly rejoice
that he lived at a time to see this fair country discovered
and settled; he must necessarily feel a share of national
pride, when he views the chain of settlements which em-
bellishes these extended shores. When he says to him-

[9] Reprinted from the American Edition of 1793.

self, this is the work of my countrymen, who, when convulsed by factions, afflicted by a variety of miseries and wants, restless and impatient, took refuge here. They brought along with them their national genius, to which they principally owe what liberty they enjoy, and what substance they possess. Here he sees the industry of his native country displayed in a new manner, and traces in their works the embryos of all the arts, sciences, and ingenuity which flourish in Europe. Here he beholds fair cities, substantial villages, extensive fields, an immense country filled with decent houses, good roads, orchards, meadows, and bridges, where an hundred years ago all was wild, woody, and uncultivated! What a train of pleasing ideas this fair spectacle must suggest; it is a prospect which must inspire a good citizen with most heartfelt pleasure. The difficulty consists in the manner of viewing so extensive a scene. He is arrived on a new continent; a modern society offers itself to his contemplation, different from what he had hitherto seen. It is not composed, as in Europe, of great lords who possess everything, and of a herd of people who have nothing. Here are no aristocratical families, no courts, no kings, no bishops, no ecclesiastical dominion, no invisible power giving to a few a very visible one; no great manufacturers employing thousands, no great refinements of luxury. The rich and the poor are not so far removed from each other as they are in Europe. Some few towns excepted, we are all tillers of the earth, from Nova Scotia to West Florida. We are a people of cultivators, scattered over an immense territory, communicating with each other by means of good roads and navigable rivers, united by the silken bands of mild government, all respecting the laws, without dreading their power, because they are equitable. We are all animated with the spirit of an industry which is unfettered and unrestrained, because each person works for himself. . . .

What attachment can a poor European emigrant have for a country where he had nothing? The knowledge of the language, the love of a few kindred as poor as himself, were the only cords that tied him: his country is now that which gives him land, bread, protection, and consequence: *Ubi panis ibi patria,* is the motto of all emigrants. What then is the American, this new man? He is either an European, or the descendant of an European, hence that strange mixture of blood, which you will find in no other country. I could point out to you a family whose grandfather was an Englishman, whose wife was Dutch, whose son married a French woman, and whose present four sons have now four wives of different nations. He is an American, who, leaving behind him all his ancient prejudices and manners, receives new ones from the new mode of life he has embraced, the new government he obeys, and the new rank he holds. He becomes an American by being received in the broad lap of our great *Alma Mater*. Here individuals of all nations are melted into a new race of men, whose labours and posterity will one day cause great changes in the world. Americans are the western pilgrims, who are carrying along with them that great mass of arts, sciences, vigour, and industry which began long since in the east; they will finish the great circle. The Americans were once scattered all over Europe; here they are incorporated into one of the finest systems of population which has ever appeared, and which will hereafter become distinct by the power of the different climates they inhabit. The Americans ought therefore to love this country much better than that wherein either he or his forefathers were born. Here the rewards of his industry follow the equal steps the progress of his labour; his labour is founded on the basis of nature, *self-interest;* can it want a stronger allurement? Wives and children, who before in vain demanded of him a morsel of bread, now, fat and frolicsome, gladly help their father to clear those fields whence exuberant crops are to arise to feed and to clothe them all; without any part being claimed, either by a despotic prince, a rich abbot, or a mighty lord. Here religion demands but little of him; a small voluntary salary to the minister, and gratitude to God; can he refuse these? The American is a new man, who acts upon new principles; he must therefore entertain new ideas, and form new opinions. From involuntary idleness, servile dependence, penury, and useless labour, he has passed to toils of a very different nature, rewarded by ample subsistence.—This is an American. . . .

— Document No. 10 —

INTERNAL IMPROVEMENTS [10]

Early nationalist America sought the quick opening of the country and realized that, in the speeding of the process, public support was necessary. The federal government was called upon to participate and did so until President Jackson put an end to federal assistance in his Maysville bill veto of 1830. The states then embarked on their programs of financing, most of these ending disastrously during the depression of 1837-43. The federal government did not re-enter the scene until the Civil War, when it began to aid the construction of transcontinental railroads. Henry Clay, congressman and senator from Kentucky, was one of the early advocates of internal improvements; the selection is from a speech in the House in 1818.

✓   ✓   ✓

Some principles drawn from political economists have been alluded to, and we are advised to leave things to themselves, upon the ground that, when the condition of society is ripe for internal improvements—that is, when capital can be so invested with a fair prospect of adequate remuneration, they will be executed by associations of individuals, unaided by government. With my friend from South Carolina (Mr. Lowndes) I concur in this as a general maxim; and I also concur with him that there are exceptions to it. . . . In regard to internal improvements, it does not follow that they will always be constructed whenever they will afford a competent dividend upon the capital invested. It may be true, generally, that in old countries where there is a great accumulation of surplus capital, and a consequent low rate of interest, they will be made. But, in

[10] *Works of Henry Clay*, Calvin Colton, ed., 6 vols. (New York, 1857), vol. V.

a new country, the condition of society may be ripe for
public works long before there is, in the hands of individuals, the necessary accumulation of capital to effect
them; and besides, there is, generally, in such a country,
not only a scarcity of capital, but such a multiplicity of
profitable objects presenting themselves as to distract
the judgment. Further; the aggregate benefit resulting to
the whole society, from a public improvement, may be
such as to amply justify the investment of capital in its
execution, and yet that benefit may be so distributed
among different and distant persons that they can never
be got to act in concert. The turnpike roads wanted to
pass the Alleghany mountains, and the Delaware and
Chesapeake Canal are objects of this description. Those
who will be most benefited by these improvements reside
at a considerable distance from the sites of them; many
of those persons never have seen and never will see them.
How is it possible to regulate the contributions, or to
present to individuals so situated a sufficiently lively pic-
ture of their real interests, to get them to make exertions in effectuating the object commensurate with their
respective abilities? I think it very possible that the
capitalist who should invest his money in one of these
objects, might not be reimbursed three per centum
annually upon it; and yet society, in various forms, might
actually reap fifteen or twenty per centum. The benefit
resulting from a turnpike road, made by private association, is divided between the capitalist who receives his
tolls, the lands through which it passes, and which are
augmented in their value, and the commodities whose
value is enhanced by the diminished expense of transportation. . . .

Again, improvements, made by private associations,
are generally made by local capital. But ages must elapse
before there will be concentrated in certain places, where
the interests of the whole community may call for improvements, sufficient capital to make them. The place
of the improvement, too, is not always the most interested in its accomplishment. Other parts of the Union—
the whole line of the seaboard—are quite as much, if
not more interested, in the Delaware and Chesapeake
Canal, as the small tract of country through which it is
proposed to pass. The same observation will apply to

turnpike roads passing through the Alleghany mountain. Sometimes the interest of the place of the improvement is adverse to the improvement and to the general interest. I would cite Louisville, at the rapids of the Ohio, as an example, whose interest will probably be more promoted by the continuance, than the removal of the obstruction. . . .

— Document No. 11 —

FINANCING THE EARLY RAILROADS[11]

Pre-Civil War America, from 1840 to 1860, gave a good deal of attention to the question of railroad building. Financing them was important, for the United States was still a poor country. H. V. Poor one of the early American railroad authorities, described the problem of financing eastern lines, where the country was already built up. D. A. Neal, one of the directors of the Illinois Central Railroad, wrote to attract capital into that great venture, which was to open up new country.

✔   ✔   ✔

I

Where there are no manufacturing establishments upon a route, the movement of property upon New England roads is limited, and hence the comparative unproductiveness of what may be termed *agricultural* lines. In the

[11] H. V. Poor in I. D. Andrews, "Report on Trade and Commerce," 32 Congress 1 Session. *H. Ex. Doc.,* No. 136 (Washington 1853); *Documents Relating to the Organization of the Illinois Central Rail-road Company* (New York, 1851).

eastern States other sources of business make up for
the lack of agricultural products for transportation, and
the aggregate investment is productive. In the southern
and western States the soil supplies a very large surplus
for exportation, affording often, per mile, a greater *bulk*
for transportation than is supplied to eastern roads,
either from agriculture, manufacture, or commerce. The
cost of the former, however, will not on the average,
equal one-half that of the latter; and as the rates of
charges are pretty uniform upon all, and if anything
higher upon the *southern* and *western* than upon the
eastern roads, the revenues of the former must of course
be very much greater than the latter. Such is the fact.
The greater income of the one results, both from a larger
traffic, which the western country in particular in adapted
to supply, and from the higher rates of charges in proportion to the cost of the respective lines of the two different sections of the country. Numerous illustrations
of this fact might be readily given. The earnings of the
Cleveland and Columbus road have been greater than
those of the Hudson river since the opening of their respective lines, though the former is only 135 miles long
and cost $3,000,000, while the latter is 144 miles and
cost $10,000,000. Railroads in the newly settled por-
tions of the country, as a general rule, command a much
larger traffic, and of course yield a better return upon
their cost, than those of the older States. . . .

By far the greater number of our roads in progress
are in the interior of the country—in our agricultural dis-
tricts, that do not possess an amount of *accumulated*
capital equal to their cost. A business adequate to the
support of a railroad may exist without the means to
construct one. The construction of a railroad, too, creates opportunities for investment which promise a much
greater return than the stock in such a work. While,
therefore, our people are disposed to make every reason-
able sacrifice to secure a railroad, they prefer, and in
fact they find it more for their interest, to borrow a
portion of the amount required, than to invest the whole
means directly in the project. They can better afford to
secure the co-operation of foreign capital, by offering
high premiums for its use, than to embarrass themselves

by making a permanent investment of too large a proportion of their own immediate means. These facts sufficiently explain the reasons why the borrowing of a considerable portion of the cost of our roads has become so universal a rule.

It is only by the co-operation of capitalists residing at a distance, and having no interest in the collateral advantages due to railroads, that the great majority of our works could have been constructed. . . .

II

The Illinois Central Rail Road Company has been organized, the Capital Stock subscribed, and twenty per cent. of it paid in, all the conditions of the Charter have been complied with, and all the deeds, grants and trusts executed. Engineers are employed in selecting a route and the donated lands, which will amount to 3840 acres for each mile of road, or in the aggregate (the Road and Branches being assumed at 670 miles) 2,572,800 acres.

It is proposed to meet the cost of construction by the issue of Bonds, payable in 1875, bearing interest not exceeding seven per cent. The security for the principal will be—1st, the Road itself; and 2d, two million acres of the donated lands. The security for the interest will be 1st, the Capital Stock; 2d, the Income of the Road; 3d, two hundred and fifty thousand acres of the land specially appropriated.

The lands will be valued at prices that will more than cover any possible amount required for construction, but which, it is believed, will be fully realized before the period of the maturity of the Bonds. These Bonds may, at any time, be surrendered and any land on sale claimed in lieu of them at the appraisement. None of the lands appropriated for their security, can be disposed of, except on the simultaneous surrender or payment of Bonds to an amount equal to their appraisal. That appraisal of the two millions of acres mortgaged for their security, that is, the price under which they will not be sold, and to which it is expected they will advance at some time previous to 1875, will be so arranged, as soon as they are selected and their character known, as to produce the following averages.

400,000	acres ordinary agricultural lands $6,	$ 2,400,000
1,200,000	acres good agricultural lands $10,	12,000,000
300,000	acres superior agricultural lands $15,	4,500,000
100,000	acres town sites, mineral lands $25,	2,500,000
2,000,000		$21,400,000

To enable the Company to meet the demand for these lands at any time, short of the period of the maturity of the Bonds, the right to anticipate their payment has been reserved, but only on condition of giving one hundred and twenty dollars for every hundred so taken up.

During the time occupied in the construction of the Road, the interest on the outlay will be included in its cost. Immediately on its completion, the Income, after paying current expenses and State tax, will be of course applied to this object. If it should not, at first, be sufficient, the earnings from any partial use of the road, before its entire completion, the whole capital stock of the Company, and the entire proceeds of sales of 250,000 acres of land set aside for this purpose, will form a fund that will be ample under any contingency. . . .

The sources of income will be found,

1st. In the produce of the mines and forests, for these furnish articles ready for use and of general consumption every where.

2d. In the produce of the soil, which requires easy and cheap transportation to induce as much as it does sunshine and rain, to perfect its cultivation.

3d. In the supplies requisite to those who may be engaged in occupations connected with or incident to the two above named branches of business.

4th. In the movements of the same persons for purposes of business or pleasure.

5th. In the transit of persons and goods between points beyond the limits of the State for which the route will afford the most convenient and expeditious passage.

6th. In transportation of mails and expresses, and in other miscellaneous operations.

— Document No. 12 —

EARLY MANUFACTURES[12]

*As early as 1814, New England merchants, who had
made their fortunes in the China and India trades, turned
their attention to the erection of cotton manufactures in
the United States. Freeman Hunt, one of the first American publicists and editors to be concerned with business
enterprise, began to recite the tales of these early industrial ventures in his* Merchants' Magazine. *Many of these
writings were collected in his* Lives of American Merchants; *this selection had to do with Francis C. Lowell.*

    ✓   ✓   ✓

Mr. Lowell had just returned to this country, after a
long visit to England and Scotland. While abroad, he had
conceived the idea that the cotton manufacture, then
almost monopolized by Great Britain, might be advan-
tageously prosecuted here. The use of machinery was
daily superseding the former manual operations; and it
was known that power-looms had recently been introduced, though the mode of constructing them was kept
secret. The cheapness of labor, and abundance of capital,
were advantages in favor of the English manufacturer—
they had skill and reputation. On the other hand, they
were burdened with the taxes of a prolonged war. We
could obtain the raw material cheaper, and had a great
superiority in the abundant water-power, then unemployed, in every part of New England. It was also the
belief of Mr. Lowell, that the character of our population, educated, moral, and enterprising as it then was,
could not fail to secure success, when brought into competition with their European rivals; and it is no small
evidence of the farreaching views of this extraordinary

[12] *Lives of American Merchants,* 2 vols. (New York, 1856-
58), vol. I.

man, and his early colleagues, that their very first measures were such as should secure that attention to education and morals among the manufacturing population, which they believed to be the corner-stone of any permanent success. . . .

The first object to be accomplished, was to procure a power-loom. To obtain one from England was, of course, impracticable; and, although there were many patents for such machines in our Patent Office, not one had yet exhibited sufficient merit to be adopted into use. Under these circumstances, but one resource remained—to invent one themselves; and this these earnest men at once set about. Unacquainted as they were with machinery, in practice, they dared, nevertheless, to attempt the solution of a problem that had baffled the most ingenious mechanicians. In England, the power-loom had been invented by a clergyman, and why not here by a merchant? After numerous experiments and failures, they at last succeeded, in the autumn of 1812, in producing a model which they thought so well of as to be willing to make preparations for putting up a mill, for the weaving of cotton cloth. . . .

Great difficulty was at first experienced at Waltham, for the want of a proper preparation (sizing) of the warps. They procured from England a drawing of Horrock's dressing-machine, which, with some essential improvements, they adopted, producing the dresser now in use at Lowell and elsewhere. No method was, however, indicated in this drawing for winding the threads from the bobbins on to the beam; and to supply this deficiency, Mr. Moody invented the very ingenious machine called the warper. Having obtained these, there was no further difficulty in weaving by power-looms.

There was still greater deficiency in the preparation for spinning. They had obtained from England a description of what was then called a bobbin and fly, or jack-frame, for spinning roving; from this Mr. Moody and Mr. Lowell produced our present double-speeder. The motions of this machine were very complicated, and required nice mathematical calculations. Without them, Mr. Moody's ingenuity, great as it was, would have been at fault. These were supplied by Mr. Lowell. . . .

There was also great waste and expense in winding the thread for filling or weft from the bobbin on to the quills, for the shuttle. To obviate this, Mr. Moody invented the machine known here as the filling-throstle.

It will be seen, by this rapid sketch, how much there was at this early period to be done, and how well it was accomplished. The machines introduced then, are those still in use in New England—brought, of course, to greater perfection in detail, and attaining a much higher rate of speed, but still substantially the same.

Associating with themselves some of the most intelligent merchants of Boston, they procured, in February, 1813, a charter, under the name of the Boston Manufacturing Company, with a capital of one hundred thousand dollars. Success crowned their efforts, and the business was gradually extended to the limit of the capacity of their water-power. . . .

By the erection of boarding-houses at the expense and under the control of the factory; putting at the head of them matrons of tried character, and allowing no boarders to be received except the female operatives of the mill; by stringent regulations for the government of these houses; by all these precautions they gained the confidence of the rural population, who were now no longer afraid to trust their daughters in a manufacturing town. A supply was thus obtained of respectable girls; and these, from pride of character, as well as principle, have taken especial care to exclude all others. . . .

— Document No. 13 —

TWO SOUTHERNERS LOOK AT SLAVERY [13]

[13] George Fitzhugh, *Cannibals All!; or, Slaves Without Masters* (Richmond, 1857); Hinton R. Helper, *The Impending Crisis* (New York, 1860).

The Virginian George Fitzhugh, in his Cannibals All!, *his defense of Negro slavery, sought to demonstrate that slavery, as a capitalist institution, was more humane than the "white slavery" of northern industrialism. The North Carolinian Hinton R. Helper, in his* The Impending Crisis, *attacked slavery because, to him, its leading victims were the "poor whites"—the large, non-slave-owning masses— of the South. The selections are from both these very influential books.*

✓   ✓   ✓

I

Probably, you are a lawyer, or a merchant, or a doctor, who have made by your business fifty thousand dollars, and retired to live on your capital. But, mark! not to spend your capital. That would be vulgar, disreputable, criminal. That would be, to live by your own labor; for your capital is your amassed labor. That would be, to do as common working men do; for they take the pittance which their employers leave them, to live on. They live by labor; for they exchange the results of their own labor for the products of other people's labor. It is, no doubt, an honest, vulgar way of living; but not at all a respectable way. The respectable way of living is, to make other people work for you, and to pay them nothing for so doing—and to have no concern about them after their work is done. Hence, white slaveholding is much more respectable than negro slavery—for the master works nearly as hard for the negro, as he for the master. But you, my virtuous, respectable reader, exact three thousand dollars per annum from white labor, (for your income is the product of white labor,) and make not one cent of return in any form. You retain your capital, and never labor, and yet live in luxury on the labor of others. Capital commands labor, as the master does the slave. Neither pays for labor; but the master permits the slave to retain a larger allowance from the proceeds of his own labor, and hence "free labor is cheaper than slave labor." You, with the command over labor which your capital gives you, are a slave owner —a master, without the obligations of a master. They who work for you, who create your income, are slaves, without the rights of slaves. Slaves without a master! Whilst you were engaged in amassing your capital, in seeking to become independent, you were in the White Slave Trade. . . .

The negro slaves of the South are the happiest, and, in some sense, the freest people in the world. The children and the aged and infirm work not at all, and yet have all the comforts and necessaries of life provided for them. They enjoy liberty, because they are oppressed neither by care nor labor. The women do little hard work, and are protected from the despotism of their husbands by their masters. The negro men and stout boys work, on the average, in good weather, not more than nine hours a day. The balance of their time is spent in perfect abandon. . . . We do not know whether free laborers ever sleep. They are fools to do so; for, whilst they sleep, the wily and watchful capitalist is devising means to ensnare and exploitate them. The free laborer must work or starve. He is more of a slave than the negro, because he works longer and harder for less allowance than the slave, and has no holiday, because the cares of life with him begin when its labors end. He has no liberty, and not a single right. . . .

Free laborers have not a thousandth part of the rights and liberties of negro slaves. Indeed, they have not a single right or a single liberty, unless it be the right or liberty to die. But the reader may think that he and other capitalists and employers are freer than negro slaves. Your capital would soon vanish, if you dared indulge in the liberty and abandon of negroes. You hold your wealth and position by the tenure of constant watchfulness, care and circumspection. You never labor; but you are never free. . . .

II

Notwithstanding the fact that the white non-slave-holders of the South, are in the majority, as five to one, they have never yet had any part or lot in framing the laws under which they live. There is no legislation except for the benefit of slavery, and slaveholders. As a general rule, poor white persons are regarded with less esteem and attention than negroes, and though the condition of the latter is wretched beyond description, vast numbers of the former are infinitely worse off. A cunningly devised mockery of freedom is guaranteed to them, and that is all. To all intents and purposes they are disfranchised, and outlawed, and the only privilege extended to them, is a shallow and circumscribed participation in the political movements that usher slaveholders into office.

We have not breathed away seven and twenty years in the South, without becoming acquainted with the demagogical manoeuvrings of the oligarchy. Their intrigues and tricks of legerdemain are as familiar to us as household words; in vain might the world be ransacked for a more precious junto of flatterers and cajolers. It is amusing to ignorance, amazing to credulity, and insulting to intelligence, to hear them in their blattering efforts to mystify and pervert the sacred principles of liberty, and turn the curse of slavery into a blessing. To the illiterate poor whites—made poor and ignorant by the system of slavery—they hold out the idea that slavery is the very bulwark of our liberties, and the foundation of American independence! For hours at a time, day after day, will they expatiate upon the inexpressible beauties and excellencies of this great, *free* and *independent* nation; and finally, with the most extravagant gesticulations and rhetorical flourishes, conclude their nonsensical ravings, by attributing all the glory and prosperity of the country, from Maine to Texas, and from Georgia to California, to the "invaluable institutions of the South!" With what patience we could command, we have frequently listened to the incoherent and truthmurdering declamations of these champions of slavery, and, in the absence of a more politic method of giving vent to our disgust and indignation, have involuntarily bit our lips into blisters.

— Document No. 14 —

DEFENSE OF ACCUMULATION[14]

*The extraordinary burgeoning of industrial capitalism
in the post-Civil War period naturally attracted the attention of thoughtful Americans, many of whom specu-
lated on its causes and consequences. Two such were
William Graham Sumner (1840-1910) and Andrew
Carnegie (1835-1919) who, coming from different back-
grounds and accomplishments, arrived at somewhat similar conclusions. Sumner was a professor at Yale; Carnegie was the founder of the great Carnegie Steel Company. Both saw in private enterprise the great hope of
America. Sumner espoused a completely laissez-faire
policy by the state and assumed progress if individuals
were left unhampered; Carnegie agreed, but went a step
further in calling upon the wealthy to use their fortunes
wisely for social purposes. The first selection is from
Summer's* What Social Classes Owe to Each Other;
*the second from an address Carnegie delivered in Janu-
ary, 1895.*

✓   ✓   ✓

I

It is commonly asserted that there are in the United
States no classes, and any allusion to classes is resented.
On the other hand, we constantly read and hear discussions of social topics in which the existence of social
classes is assumed as a simple fact. "The poor," "the
weak," "the laborers," are expressions which are used
as if they had exact and well-understood definition. . . .

There is no possible definition of a "poor man." A
pauper is a person who cannot earn his living; whose
producing powers have fallen positively below his neces-

[14] W. G. Sumner, *What Social Classes Owe to Each Other*
(New York, 1883); Andrew Carnegie, *Wealth and Its
Uses* (New York).

sary consumption; who cannot, therefore, pay his way. A human society needs the active co-operation and productive energy of every person in it. A man who is present as a consumer, yet who does not contribute either by land, labor, or capital to the work of society, is a burden. On no sound political theory ought such a person to share in the political power of the State. He drops out of the ranks of workers and producers. Society must support him. It accepts the burden, but he must be cancelled from the ranks of the rulers likewise. So much for the pauper. About him no more need be said. But he is not the "poor man." The "poor man" is an elastic term, under which any number of social fallacies may be hidden. . . .

The humanitarians, philanthropists, and reformers, looking at the facts of life as they present themselves, find enough which is sad and unpromising in the condition of many members of society. They see wealth and poverty side by side. They note great inequality of social position and social chances. They eagerly set about the attempt to account for what they see, and to devise schemes for remedying what they do not like. In their eagerness to recommend the less fortunate classes to pity and consideration they forget all about the rights of other classes; they gloss over all the faults of the classes in question, and they exaggerate their misfortunes and their virtues. They invent new theories of property, distorting rights and perpetrating injustice, as any one is sure to do who sets about the re-adjustment of social relations with the interests of one group distinctly before his mind, and the interests of all other groups thrown into the background. When I have read certain of these discussions I have thought that it must be quite disreputable to be respectable, quite dishonest to own property, quite unjust to go one's own way and earn one's own living, and that the only really admirable person was the good-for-nothing. The man who by his own effort raises himself above poverty appears, in these discussions, to be of no account. The man who has done nothing to raise himself above poverty finds that the social doctors flock about him, bringing the capital which they have collected from the other class, and promising him the aid of the State to give him what the other had

to work for. In all these schemes and projects the organized intervention of society through the State is either
planned or hoped for, and the State is thus made to become the protector and guardian of certain classes. . . .

II

The principal complaint against our industrial conditions of to-day is that they cause great wealth to flow
into the hands of the few. Well, of the very few, indeed,
is this true. It was formerly so, as I have explained, immediately after the new inventions had changed the conditions of the world. To-day it is not true. Wealth is
being more and more distributed among the many. The
amount of the combined profits of labour and capital
which goes to labour was never so great as to-day, the
amount going to capital never so small. While the earnings of capital have fallen more than one-half, in many
cases have been entirely obliterated, statistics prove that
the earnings of labour were never so high as they were
previous to the recent unprecedented depression in business, while the cost of living,—the necessaries of life,—
have fallen in some cases nearly one-half. . . .

You may be sure, gentlemen, that the question of the
distribution of wealth is settling itself rapidly under
present conditions, and settling itself in the right direction. The few rich are getting poorer, and the toiling
masses are getting richer. Nevertheless, a few exceptional
men may yet make fortunes, but these will be more
moderate than in the part. This may not be quite as
fortunate for the masses of the people as is now believed, because great accumulations of wealth in the
hands of one enterprising man who still toils on are
sometimes most productive of all forms of wealth. Take
the richest man the world ever saw, who died in New
York some years ago. What was found in his case? That,
with the exception of a small percentage used for daily
expenses, his entire fortune and all its surplus earnings
were invested in enterprises which developed the railway
system of our country, which gives to the people the
cheapest transportation known. Whether the millionnaire
wishes it or not, he cannot evade the law which under
present conditions compels him to use his millions for
the good of the people. All that he gets during the few

years of his life is that he may live in a finer house, surround himself with finer furniture, and works of art which may be added: he could even have a grander library, more of the gods around him; but, as far as I have known millionnaires, the library is the least used part of what he would probably consider "furniture" in all his mansion. He can eat richer food and drink richer wines, which only hurt him. But truly the modern millionnaire is generally a man of very simple tastes and even miserly habits. He spends little upon himself, and is the toiling bee laying up the honey in the industrial hive, which all the inmates of that hive, the community in general, will certainly enjoy. . . .

The inventions of to-day lead to concentrating industrial and commercial affairs into huge concerns. You cannot work the Bessemer process successfully without employing thousands of men upon one spot. You could not make the armour for ships without first expending seven millions of dollars, as the Bethlehem Company has spent. You cannot make a yard of cotton goods in competition with the world without having an immense factory and thousands of men and women aiding in the process. The great electric establishment here in your town succeeds because it has spent millions, and is prepared to do its work upon a great scale. Under such conditions it is impossible but that wealth will flow into the hands of a few men in prosperous times beyond their needs. But out of fifty great fortunes which Mr. Blaine had a list made of he found only one man who was reputed to have made a large fortune in manufacturing. These are made from real estate more than from all other causes combined; next follows transportation, banking. The whole manufacturing world furnished but one millionaire. . . .

— Document No. 15 —

RAILROAD ABUSES[15]

[15] *First Annual Report of the Interstate Commerce Commission* (Washington, D. C., 1887), pp. 1-9.

After almost two decades of agitation and attempted State regulation, Congress finally was impelled to pass the Interstate Commerce Act in 1887. This was the federal government's first attempt to interfere with the conduct of business; from thence on, moving slowly in the next two decades and then with increasing speed under the New Freedom and the New Deal, government penetrated into every area of the country's economic life. The Interstate Commerce Commission, in its first report, recited some of the abuses in railroading that led to federal regulation.

✓   ✓   ✓

The system of making special arrangements with shippers was in many parts of the country not confined to large manufacturers and dealers, but was extended from person to person under the pressure of alleged business necessity, or because of personal importunity or favoritism, and even in some cases from a desire to relieve individuals from the consequences of previous unfair concessions to rivals in business. The result was that shipments of importance were commonly made under special bargains entered into for the occasion, or to stand until revoked, of which the shipper and the representative of the road were the only parties having knowledge. These arrangements took the form of special rates, rebates, and drawbacks, underbilling, reduced classification, or whatever might be best adapted to keep the transaction from the public; but the public very well understood that private arrangements were to be had if the proper motives were presented. The memorandum-book carried in the pocket of the general freight agent often contained the only record of the rates made to the different patrons of the road, and it was in his power to place a man or a community under an immense obligation by conceding a special rate on one day, and to nullify the effect of it on the next by doing even better by a competitor. . . .

Whatever was the motive, the allowance of the special rate or rebate was essentially unjust and corrupting; it wronged the smaller dealer, oftentimes to an extent that was ruinous, and it was very generally accompanied by an allowance of free personal transportation to the larger dealer, which had the effect to emphasize its evils. There was not the least doubt that had the case been properly brought to a judicial test these transactions would in many cases have been held to be illegal at the common law; but the proof was in general difficult, against the party which fixed the rates of transportation at pleasure, as has already been explained, might prove more injurious than the rebate itself. . . .

The inevitable result was that this management of the business had a direct and very decided tendency to strengthen unjustly the strong among the customers and to depress the weak. These were very great evils, and the indirect consequences were even greater and more pernicious than the direct, for they tended to fix in the public mind a belief that injustice and inequality in the employment of public agencies were not condemned by the law, and that success in business was to be sought for in favoritism rather than in legitimate competition and enterprise. . . .

— Document No. 16 —

AGRARIAN UNREST [16]

As prices for agricultural commodities declined, following the crisis of 1873, Western and Southern farmers became increasingly restive. They saw their problems in financial terms and they singled out the banking community as the farmer's chief foe. More and more, agriculture talked of money; it was no accident, therefore, that the Populist Party should be captured in 1896 by William Jennings Bryan with his platform of "Free Silver." Senator William A. Peffer (1831-1912) of Kansas was a leading Populist; the document presented here was a characteristic statement of the Populist position.

[16] William A. Peffer, *The Farmer's Side* (New York, 1891).

✔   ✔   ✔

From this array of testimony the reader need have no difficulty in determining for himself "how we got here." The hand of the money changer is upon us. Money dictates our financial policy; money controls the business of the country; money is despoiling the people. The author of *Twenty-eight Years in Wall Street* boasts that in the wonderful commercial and industrial development of the age, and which, he says, exceeds that of all past time since Herodotus wrote, Wall Street was a prime factor. He claims, and truthfully too, that the power of the men who assemble there to catch the driftwood of trade is greater than that of monarchies. He says they "move the money which controls the affairs of the world." We see plainly that behind all the commercial villainies of the time this power rests in placid security while the robbing of the toilers proceeds. These men of Wall Street, posing as missionaries conquering deserts and building republics, men piously assuming universal dominion, religiously dictating the financial policies of nations, moving in an atmosphere of radiant morals, self-appointed philosophers teaching honor and honesty to an ignorant world, these men of fabulous fortunes built upon the ruin of their fellows, are in fact the most audacious gamblers in Christendom. The poor fool who with a few dollars opens a faro bank or sets up a monte table in a country town is by common consent an outlaw; every man's face is set against him, and he is liable to arrest and imprisonment at any hour; he is denied admittance to the houses of people who are clean; even the street gamins pass him by as if he were a leper. No man so little esteemed, no man so thoroughly loathed and despised as this fellow, the common gambler. Yet here in the very heart of the best civilization on earth, at the very center of business life and activity, living in luxury and ease, renting costly pews in splendid churches and hiring their worshiping done; men petted and feasted by the rich and easy everywhere, with millions of dollars at their call, governments at their command, and a loyal people in their service; these men who produce nothing, who add not a dollar to the nation's wealth, who fatten on the failures of other men, whose acquisitions are only

what their fellows have lost; these men without conscience, who believe they are specially commissioned to
prey upon the people, who act as a sort of continuing
self-appointed civil-service commission to examine can-
didates for important offices before their names are submitted to the voters; this pampered aristocracy living off
the wreckage of commerce, who rake in a railroad, a
state, or a nation with equal complacency; these men
"whose private dwellings are more splendid than the
public buildings," and whose "happy homes" are the
fruit of other men's toil; these men who boast of their
patriotism in lending a few millions of their ill-gotten
gains to the government of their imperiled country at
"12 per cent" interest, when thousands of farmers and
wage workers of all sorts and conditions were voluntarily in the army at risk of life and home—all without
question as to pay; these men masquerading as philanthropists and patriots while they are despoiling a nation
and robbing the poor—these are the men who engineered
the train that brought us where we are. They hold the
bonds of nearly every State, county, city, and township
in the Union; every railroad owes them more than it is
worth. Corners in grain and other products of toil are
the legitimate fruits of Wall Street methods. Every trust
and combine made to rob the people had its origin in
the example of Wall Street dealers. Touch any spring
along the keyboard of commercial gambling and a Wall
Street sign appears. This dangerous power which money
gives is fast undermining the liberties of the people. It
now has control of nearly half their homes, and is reaching out its clutching hands for the rest. This is the power
we have to deal with. It is the giant evil of the time.
Money is the great issue—all others pale into insignifi-
cance before this, the father of them.

— Document No. 17 —

CONCENTRATION AND CONTROL [17]

American preoccupation with monopoly ran back to the founding of the Republic, when Jefferson fought against the chartering of the First Bank. Legislation was finally written in 1890 in the passage of the Sherman Antitrust Act. The effectiveness of legal officers and courts was strengthened by the work of commissions and legislative committees. An example of the latter was the so-called Pujo Committee, a committee of the lower house of Congress, which issued its report in 1913. The Pujo Committee made the center of its inquiry the concentration of the control of money and credit.

✓   ✓   ✓

SECTION 3—PROCESSES OF CONCENTRATION

This increased concentration of control of money and credit has been effected principally as follows:

First, through consolidations of competitive or potentially competitive banks and trust companies, which consolidations in turn have recently been brought under sympathetic management.

Second, through the same powerful interests becoming large stockholders in potentially competitive banks and trust companies. This is the simplest way of acquiring control, but since it requires the largest investment of capital, it is the least used, although the recent investments in that direction for that apparent purpose amount to tens of millions of dollars in present market values.

Third, through the confederation of potentially competitive banks and trust companies by means of the system of interlocking directorates.

[17] *Report of the Committee . . . to Investigate the Concentration of Control of Money and Credit,* House Report No. 1593, 62nd Cong., 3d Sess., 1913.

Fourth, through the influence which the more powerful banking houses, banks, and trust companies have secured in the management of insurance companies, railroads, producing and trading corporations, and public utility corporations, by means of stockholdings, voting trusts, fiscal agency contracts, or representation upon their boards of directors, or through supplying the money requirements of railway, industrial, and public utilities corporations and thereby being enabled to participate in the determination of their financial and business policies.

Fifth, through partnership or joint account arrangements between a few of the leading banking houses, banks, and trust companies in the purchase of security issues of the great interstate corporations, accompanied by understandings of recent growth—sometimes called "banking ethics"—which have had the effect of effectually destroying competition between such banking houses, banks, and trust companies in the struggle for business or in the purchase and sale of large issues of such securities.

SECTION 4—AGENTS OF CONCENTRATION

It is a fair deduction from the testimony that the most active agents in forwarding and bringing about the concentration of control of money and credit through one or another of the processes above described have been and are—

J. P. Morgan & Co.
First National Bank of New York
National City Bank of New York
Lee, Higginson & Co., of Boston and New York
Kidder, Peabody & Co., of Boston and New York
Kuhn, Loeb & Co.

Combined Power of Morgan & Co., the First National, and National City Banks. In the earlier pages of the report the power of these three great banks was separately set forth. It is now appropriate to consider their combined power as one group.

First, as regards banking resources:

The resources of Morgan & Co. are unknown; its deposits are $163,000,000. The resources of the First National Bank are $150,000,000 and those of its appendage, the First Security Co., at a very low estimate, $35,000,-000. The resources of the National City Bank are $274,-000,000; those of its appendage, the National City Co., are unknown, though the capital of the latter is alone $10,000,000. Thus, leaving out of account the very considerable part which is unknown, the institutions composing this group have resources of upward of $632,-000,000, aside from the vast individual resources of Messrs. Morgan, Baker, and Stillman.

Further, as heretofore shown, the members of this group, through stockholdings, voting trusts, interlocking directorates, and other relations, have become in some cases the absolutely dominant factor, in others the most important single factor, in the control of the following banks and trust companies in the city of New York.

(a)	Bankers Trust Co., resources	$250,000,000
(b)	Guaranty Trust Co., resources	$232,000,000
(c)	Astor Trust Co., resources	$ 27,000,000
(d)	National Bank of Commerce, resources	$190,000,000
(e)	Liberty National Bank, resources	$ 29,000,000
(f)	Chase National Bank, resources	$150,000,000
(g)	Farmers Loan & Trust Co., resources	$135,000,000

in all, 7, with total resources of $968,000,000
which, added to the known resources of
members of the group themselves, makes $1,600,000,000
as the aggregate of known banking resources in the city of New York under their
control or influence.

If there be added also the resources of
the Equitable Life Assurance Society controlled through stock ownership of J. P.
Morgan $504,000,000

the amount becomes $2,104,000,000

Summary of Directorships Held by These Members of the Group. Exhibit 134-B . . . shows the combined directorships in the more important enterprises held by Morgan & Co., the First National Bank, the National City Bank, and the Bankers and Guaranty Trust Cos., Morgan & Co. through voting trusts. It appears there that firm members of directors of these institutions together hold:

One hundred and eighteen directorships in 34 banks and trust companies having total resources of $2,679,000,000 and total deposits of $1,983,000,000.

Thirty directorships in 10 insurance companies having total assets of $2,293,000,000.

One hundred and five directorships in 32 transportation systems having a total capitalization of $11,784,000,000 and a total mileage (excluding express companies and steamship lines) of 150,200.

Sixty-three directorships in 24 producing and trading corporations having a total capitalization of $3,339,000,000.

Twenty-five directorships in 12 public utility corporations having a total capitalization of $2,150,000,000.

In all, 341 directorships in 112 corporations having aggregate resources or capitalization of $22,245,000,000.

The members of the firm of J. P. Morgan & Co. held 72 directorships in 47 of the greater corporations: George F. Baker, chairman of the board, F. L. Hine, president, and George F. Baker, Jr., and C. D. Norton, vice-presidents, of the First National Bank of New York, hold 46 directorships in 37 of the greater corporations; and James Stillman, chairman of the board, Frank A. Vanderlip, president, and Samuel McRoberts, J. T. Talbert, W. A. Simonson, vice-presidents, of the National City Bank of New York, hold 32 directorships in 26 of the greater corporations; making in all for these members of the group 150 directorships in 110 of the greater corporations.

— Document No. 18 —

CONDITION OF LABOR[18]

[18] *Report on Conditions of Employment in the Iron and Steel Industry in the United States,* 62nd Congr., 1st Sess., Senate Document No. 110, vol. 1, pp. xiv-xvii.

While the United States was making impressive progress in the first decade of the 20th century, increasing production and productivity, there is reason to assume that real wages did not rise; possibly, they declined. In any case, it was short-sighted policy to overlook the latent purchasing power of the American public, notably for durable consumer goods, through improvement in working conditions and wages. The document following points up the position of labor in the United States in 1910 in the great iron and steel industry.

The fact that stands out most strikingly in any study of the labor conditions in the iron and steel industry in the United States is the unusually long schedule of working hours to which the larger number of the employees in this industry are subject.

During May, 1910, the period covered by this investigation, 50,000, or 29 per cent, of the 173,000 employees of blast furnaces and steel works and rolling mills covered by this report customarily worked 7 days per week, and 20 per cent of them worked 84 hours or more per week, which, in effect, means a 12-hour working day every day in the week, including Sunday. . . .

The hardship of a 12-hour day and a 7-day week is still further increased by the fact that every week or two weeks, as the case may be, when the employees on the day shift are transferred to the night shift, and vice versa, employees remain on duty without relief either 18 or 20 consecutive hours, according to the practice adopted for the change of shift. The most common plan to effect this change of shift is to work one shift of employees on the day of change through the entire 24 hours, the succeeding shift working the regular 12 hours when it comes on duty. . . .

That much of the Sunday labor which has been prevalent in the steel industry is no more necessary than in other industries is shown conclusively by the fact that at the time of the investigation made in 1910 by this Bureau into the conditions of labor in the Bethlehem Steel Works, the president of the Steel Corporation directed the rigid enforcement of a resolution adopted three years previous, cutting out a large part of Sunday work except in the blast-furnace department. Even in the blast-furnace department, where there is a metallurgical necessity for continuous operation day and night throughout 7 days of the week, there is practically nothing except the desire to economize in the expense of production that has prevented the introduction of a system that would give each employee 1 day of rest out of the 7.

Since the beginning of the present investigation, however, this matter of abolishing 7-day work for the individual employees in the blast furnaces, as well as in other departments of the industry, has received the attention of the American Iron and Steel Institute, and through a committee of that organization a plan has been proposed which gives each employee one day of rest each week. A number of the plants throughout the country have, at the instance of the Institute, adopted this plan or some modification of it, and have successfully operated it for several months. . . .

During the investigation those in charge of the plants have in their discussions with representatives of the Bureau frequently emphasized the fact that the men working these very long hours are not kept busy all the time. To a considerable extent this is perfectly true; but the employees in question are on duty and subject to orders during the entire period, and they are not, except in rare instances, allowed to leave the plant. It should not be overlooked that it is not simply the character or the continuity of the work but the fact that in the case of the 12-hour-a-day man one-half of each 24 hours— more than three-fourths of his waking hours—is spent on duty in the mills, which is of significance to the worker and his family. Nothing has been done by the manufacturers nor have any proposals been made to lessen the proportion of men working 72 hours or more per week. It was found in this investigation that nearly 43 per cent of the 173,000 employees in the iron and steel industry were working at least 72 hours per week, or 12 hours per day for 6 days a week. This proportion remains unchanged, being unaffected by the plan to give the men who were working 84 hours per week one day of rest in seven.

An added significance attached to the conditions of

labor here described as characteristic of the iron and steel industry when we consider that the general tendency in other industries for years past has been toward a shorter working-day. Years ago the 10 hour day became almost a standard; since that time further reductions have brought the working-day to 9, and in many cases, to 8 hours, and this reduction has been accompanied by a part holiday on Saturday. It is, therefore, in striking contrast to this general tendency in other industries to find in a great basic industry, such as that part of the iron and steel industry covered in this report, that approximately only 14 per cent of the 173,000 employees work less than 60 hours per week and almost 43 per cent work 72 hours or over per week. . . .

Of the total of 172,706 employees, 13,868, or 8.03 per cent, earned less than 14 cents per hour, 20,527, or 11.89 per cent, earned 14 and under 16 cents, and 51,417, or 29.77 per cent, earned 16 and under 18 cents. Thus 85,812, or 49.69 per cent of all the employees, received less than 18 cents per hour. Those earning 18 and under 25 cents per hour number 46,132, or 26.71 per cent, while 40,762, or 23.61 per cent, earned 25 cents and over. A few very highly skilled employees received $1.25 per hour, and those receiving 50 cents and over per hour numbered 4.403 or 2.55 per cent of all employees.

— Document No. 19 —

HOW AMERICAN BUSINESS GREW [19]

[19] Ralph W. Hidy and Muriel E. Hidy, *Pioneering in Big Business. History of Standard Oil Company* (*New Jersey*) *1882-1911* (New York, 1955), pp. 713-16. Reprinted by permission of Harper & Brothers.

Starting from modest beginnings, heavy industry in the United States grew to amazing proportions in two generations. The most significant capital contribution came from ploughed-back profits, for companies were closely held and policies were guided by owners-managers. Steel and petroleum products were the leaders and, therefore, the Carnegie Steel Company (later furnishing the basis of the United States Steel Corporation) and the various Standard Oil Companies (dominated by John D. Rockefeller) in little tell the story of American industrial expansion. Rockefeller and his partners started their oil refining business in Cleveland in the 1870s with a capitalization of less that $1 million; in 1911, their companies had a net value of $660,452,000. Professor and Mrs. Hidy tell the story of Standard's growth.

✓   ✓   ✓

The net value of Jersey Standard properties far outranked that of any separated company. As of December 21, 1911, the net value of all properties formerly in the Standard Oil combination was estimated at $660,452,000. Of this, Jersey Standard and its remaining affiliates owned $285,532,000. New York Standard stood second with $60,024,000, and The Ohio Oil Company third with $44,052,000. That the Jersey Company came out of the dismembering process so well was attributable in part to the many transfers of subsidiaries from the nineteen sister companies taken over in 1899, in part to new construction and corporate creations after 1906, and in part to the carelessness of the Attorney General's office in drawing up the original bill for breaking up the combination. It was unfortunate, but relatively unimportant, that Jersey Standard had few trade-marks registered in its own name and that it lost the advantage of such joint efforts of the combination as the research on "cracking" petroleum at Whiting. . . .

By 1911 time had tested several managerial techniques to the satisfaction of Standard Oil officials. Prominent among these was decision making by consultation and agreement through committees of executives. . . . Innovations in administrative techniques, as well as in methods of production and manufacturing, were at the root of the organization's success.

Several general policies had contributed to the efficient and profitable operation of Standard Oil enterprises. Vertical integration, from the production of crude oil and the manufacture of refined products to sales to retailers, was one of the most effective methods of organizing a petroleum enterprise, a lesson that competitors were learning at the same time. Ownership of both gathering and trunk pipelines was deemed economically desirable, if not absolutely necessary, in order to assure a steady flow of raw material to relatively immovable refining plants involving large investments. Effective location of manufacturing plants was a factor of major importance to profitable operation. Dominance in manufacturing did not assure the control of all the uncertainties in the market; expansion into wholesaling at home and abroad minimized some of the variables. Since the industry was dynamic, continuous growth of the combination seemed imperative, and expansion through reinvestment of a sizable proportion of the combination's own earnings had functioned well.

Various other conclusions based on the experience of Standard Oil could almost be termed axiomatic. The economies of large-scale operations were substantial, not only in the reduction of unit costs but in a large number of other ways. A large business could finance experimentation and research, and develop by-products, more effectively than a small one. Differentiation of products helped to keep earnings at a high level as profit margins narrowed on items earlier considered basic. The various functions of the oil industry never were in balance, but integration of a large enterprise helped to minimize the maladjustments. Careful financial management of a large unit enabled executives to shift investment to the continuously developing new producing areas, new machinery, and new processes.

— Document No. 20 —

THE SOUND BASES OF
PROSPERITY [20]

*Skilled observers were prepared to assume that the
bases of prosperity in the United States were soundly
fixed. The following is a characteristic statement, coming from the universities and not from chambers of commerce or financial promoters. It appeared in the "Introduction" of a large two-volume work surveying the
American economic scene in all its aspects. The writer of
the "Introduction" was Professor Edwin F. Gay (1867-
1946), of Harvard University, who was director of the
research staff of the study.*

And so, when we look back over a century of our
own economic history for analogous periods of fairly
continuous advance, without too minute regard for the
fluctuations of the business cycles, we find certain groups
of years which have points of likeness, and also of un-
likeness, to the experience of the United States since
1922. There have been four previous periods of efflores-
cence. These correspond approximately to increases in
contemporaneous economic activity in Western Europe.
The first of the four periods of marked acceleration set
in about 1825, with the recovery from the great fall of
prices which followed the end of the Napoleonic wars,
and, although there was one sharp break in 1834, this
period of activity culminated in the boom of 1836. Then
came the prostrating panic of 1837, the western crisis

[20] *Recent Economic Changes in the United States: Report
of the Committee on Recent Economic Changes of the
President's Conference on Unemployment.* 2 vols. (New
York, 1929). Reprinted by permission of McGraw-Hill
Book Co., Inc.

of 1839, and years of depression. Again from about 1849 to the panic of 1857, broken by a mild recession in 1854, there were successive years of unprecedented prosperity. Immediately after the Civil War there was a time of hectic prosperity and great speculative activity, but with too many disturbing factors to rank the stretch from 1865 to 1879 among the notable periods. But from 1879, through the "fat eighties," though with recessions, to 1893, we may find a third remarkable forward movement. From 1898 to the crises of 1907 there was a fourth long run of prosperity. In this case, the period of severe depression following the crisis was remarkably brief, and the country had several years of undramatic fluctuations before the curtain rose for the tragedy of the Great War.

Two of these four major periods, the second and fourth, were accompanied by new gold discoveries and rising price trends; during the first period, from 1825 to 1837, prices were gradually falling, and the third, from 1879 to 1893, experienced a marked and steady drop in prices. All of them show remarkable advances in the exploitation of the national resources, notable land occupation in the first three periods; in the last three, coal, iron and petroleum production at an accelerating rate in a world comparison, gold and silver production at a diminishing rate; in the last two periods, the other mineral resources, copper leading, came into greater prominence. With each forward surge the demand for labor has grown and immigration has responded. Despite a migration of colossal proportions, such as the world had never known, the demand for labor was nevertheless maintained. Each period saw an increase in real wages, though more lagging and less pronounced than that which we have recently witnessed. All four periods contributed notable inventions and methods for economizing and supplementing human labor. With developing pressure there was a difference in the main direction of technological advance, earlier toward transportation and horse-driven agricultural machinery, later toward industrial equipment and a great extension in the mastery and use of power. The steady growth of the vast domestic market led in each period to inevitable changes in marketing and credit organization; the "orthodox" system of distribution, with its wholesaler, local jobber, and retailer, was clearly under strain in the second period and beginning to break in the third, while new forms and relationships were being established. Each phase of activity is marked by development of the banking system to meet the demands of rapidly growing industry and commerce; and each concluding phase of crisis, 1837-1839, 1857-1860, 1893-1896, 1907, gave the impulse to banking and monetary reforms. . . .

So rapid a sketch does but faint justice to the many and complicated aspects of our economic development, and it can only indicate the answer, if answer be at all possible, to the question of similarity between our present phase and those preceding it. Fuller studies, both qualitative and quantitative not only of business cycles but of longer trends, are required, and there is reason to believe that the interest which these studies are exciting will result in more exact knowledge even of earlier periods where the source material is relatively scanty. But it will serve our present purpose to point out that most of the eight significant features of the existing economic conditions in the United States upon which we have found our foreign visitors in substantial agreement are also characteristic of former major periods of prosperity in our history. The fundamental conditions remained substantially unchanged, and the responses have therefore been similar, not so much in external form as in their essential character. Even the successive maladjustments of economic growth show, behind their external dissimilarities, and underlying likeness. . . .

— Document No. 21 —

THE BOOM[21]

[21] Ferdinand Pecora, *Wall Street Under Oath* (New York, 1939). Reprinted by permission of Simon and Schuster.

The over-expansion of the securities' market played its part in pushing the American economy of the 1920s into strange and dangerous paths. In an effort to understand the reasons for the collapse, the Senate Banking and Finance Committee, during 1933-34, investigated some of the characteristics of financial promotion. Ferdinand Pecora was the Committees' Counsel; the document is printed from his book Wall Street Under Oath, *Chapter X.*

✔   ✔   ✔

In your hands or in the writer's hands, a dollar is only a dollar. It can buy a dollar's worth of bread, or a dollar's worth of corporate stock. The skilled financier, however, would not go very far in his profession if he could not do better than that. In his hands, a dollar goes a long way: It frequently buys control of ten, or twenty, or even one hundred times as much money as the financier himself invests.

In this chapter, we shall tell the story of one of the most outstanding and spectacular examples of this process encountered during the Senate Investigation: the investments trusts of Dillon, Read and Company. . . .

Like J. P. Morgan and Company and Kuhn, Loeb and Company, Dillon, Read and Company were private bankers. They did not, however, take deposits to any considerable extent, but concentrated on the creation and sale of new securities. Here they did a huge quantity of business, issuing nearly four billion dollars of government, municipal and corporate bonds and stocks for the fifteen years following the war. This was more than Kuhn, Loeb and Company but less than J. P. Morgan and Company. . . .

This new superior technique was an amazingly simple combination of two devices; the "investment trust" and "nonvoting stock," together with some added features of Dillon, Read and Company's own invention.

The first step, taken in 1924, was the organization of a corporation known as the United States and Foreign Securities Corporation. This was to be an investment trust, i.e., a company which invests in securities, just like any private person, but with the asserted advantage of trained management and great capital resources. There were three classes of stock in the new corporation—first preferred, second preferred, and common. There were 250,000 shares of the first-named class, 50,000 shares of the second, and 1,000,000 shares of the common. The "first preferred" stock was so called because it was entitled to receive dividends of six per cent before the other classes of stock received anything, but in the matter of voting rights and control, it was anything but preferred. So long as dividends were regularly paid it could not vote at all, it had not the slightest voice in the management. It was, in short, what is known as "nonvoting stock," one of the devices which Mr. Otto Kahn had picturesquely denounced as "inventions of the devil." Under all ordinary conditions, only the common stock could vote, and therefore whoever controlled the common stock controlled the corporation.

The entire 250,000 shares of "first preferred stock" were sold to the public for $25,000,000. As an added attraction, the public was also given 250,000 shares of the common stock—one share of common with each share of first preferred. That left unsold the 50,000 shares of second preferred stock, and 750,000 shares of common stock. All of this Dillon, Read and Company bought for 5,100,-000. Thus, although it invested only one fifth as much as the public, Dillon, Read and Company, owning three fourths of the common stock, the only stock that could vote, completely controlled the corporation.

The United States and Foreign Securities Corporation, ably managed and operated during an era of rising stock prices, prospered greatly. By 1928 there was a cash surplus of $10,000,000. What had the public, who contributed $25,000,000 of the corporation's $30,000,000, gotten out of this prosperity? They had gotten their six per cent dividends on their first preferred stock—and that is all. . . .

— Document No. 22 —

DISTRESS IN AGRICULTURE[22]

There follows a more detailed analysis of agricultural decline during the 1920s, taken from Louis M. Hacker's American Problems of Today.

      ✓   ✓   ✓

Alas, boom times were all too brief and the bubble of the farmer's content was pricked with a suddenness and completeness that left him shaken to his depths. The era of deflation, which set in toward the end of 1920, left its mark on industry and agriculture alike, but whereas industry began to recover with 1922, agriculture remained permanently depressed. Land values plunged downward until in 1929, that year of golden prosperity for industry, they were not much higher than they had been before the war; crop prices dropped until, in some instances, they were lower than they had been for almost half a century; agriculture was left with a heavy burden of debt and taxation as a result of overexpansion of acreage, improvements, and public budgets. The depression of 1930 and after merely served to sharpen the outlines of a situation that had been steadily getting bleaker as the decade of the twenties progressed. Put simply, farm prices had been deflated, while farm costs— necessaries for home and field, mortgage debt, taxes— were still highly inflated. The farm account could not be balanced.

The base statistical exhibits in themselves tell a startling story. In 1919, the total farm property of the nation had been valued at $78,000,000,000; by 1929 this value was $57,604,000,000, and by 1932, $44,000,000,-000. In 1919, the total farm income was $15,000,000,-

[22] Louis M. Hacker, *American Problems of Today* (New York, 1938), pp. 115-21.

000; by 1929 $12,000,000,000, and by 1932, $5,200,-
000,000. In 1919 (with the average for 1909-1914 as
100), the prices paid by farmers for the commodities
they needed stood at 206; the prices they received, at
205, making a ratio of prices received to prices paid of
99. That is to say, the farm dollar was worth 99 cents.
But in 1929, it was worth only 89 cents; and in 1932,
only 47 cents!

The efficiency of American agriculture was being ham-
pered not only because of declines in gross and relative
income. What was more serious was the fact that fixed
charges were eating up a large and larger share of the
farmer's earnings so that he was compelled to divert the
use of income from the improvement of his techniques to
the payment of taxes and interest on mortgages. In 1910,
tax payments took 3 per cent of gross income; in 1920,
3.6 per cent; in 1930, 6 per cent. In 1910, interest on
mortgages took 3 per cent of gross income; in 1920, 4
per cent; in 1930, 6 per cent. In short, total fixed charges
absorbed 6 per cent of gross farm income in 1910 and
12 per cent in 1930: This was indeed a heavy price to
pay for land ownership. Farm mortgage debt in particular had become a millstone about the necks of American
agricultural producers. In 1910, the mortgage debt on
American farm land and buildings made up 27.3 per cent
of the value of propreties; in 1920, 29.1 per cent; and in
1930, 39.6 per cent. Inability to meet mortgage payments
and to pay taxes was converting many farm owners into
tenants or croppers or forcing them off the land altogether
to enter the industrial reserve army of America's urban
population. . . .

In 1880, 25.6 per cent of all the farms in the country
were being operated by tenants; in 1930, 42.4 per
cent. . . .

Such were the outward signs of a deep-seated malady
which was not a passing phase but had all the aspects of
permanence. Let us see what were the reasons for the
depression under which the country's agricultural interest
labored in the decades of the twenties and thirties. They
may be summed up in a single phrase: the foreign market
contracted and the domestic market did not expand.

First, as Regards the Foreign Situation. The great
historical reason for the advance of American agricul-

ture after the Civil War had been our debtor status. We were borrowing capital from Europe to help transform our capitalism from a merchant to an industrial base. As a result, we engaged in an heroic expansion of agriculture to permit payments on foreign borrowings and for those raw materials we ourselves could not produce. In brief, American industry was growing up behind high tariff walls with the assistance of foreign capital; and American agricultural surpluses helped make this possible.

By 1920 the United States had become a creditor nation. But other countries, due to the staggering costs of the World War, because they were debtors, and because of the ambitions of their own capitalists, were now desperately trying to obtain foreign exchange. How help the process better than by the enlargement of their own agricultural operations? This was notably true of the newer lands—Canada, the Latin American countries, Australasia, the Far East—which could balance their international payments only by selling in the world market those foodstuffs and fibers which we ourselves kept pouring into Europe up to the end of the World War. What made the situation worse was the fact that European countries began to strive for agricultural self-sufficiency. . . .

The result was a vast expansion in the production of agricultural goods throughout the world during the nineteen twenties. . . .

Second, as Regards the Domestic Situation. The possibilities of increasing domestic consumption of agricultural goods, in order to take in slack, were remote. The following factors may be noted: 1. Our population growth was slowing down because of immigration restriction and birth control. 2. Because of these facts, the age distribution of our population was changing, with interesting repercussions upon the consumption of agricultural goods. Indeed, the two decades 1910-1930 witnessed a profound change in dietary habits as Americans shifted from a reliance on grains and beef to a greater use of pork, vegetables, fruits, milk, and sugar. The significance of the shift lies in this fact: grains and beef are largely the products of extensive cultivation; pork products, vegetables, fruits, and milk are the products of intensive cultivation requiring less land in use and more capital expenditures. And extensive cultivation was the method of production notably of the typical American farming unit, the family farm.

Also, the consumption of agricultural goods at home was not increasing proportionately because of changing habits in feeding and clothing. 3. Women were dieting and thus eating less calories. 4. Improved methods of heating homes, the wide use of heated automobiles, and the machine's growing elimination of the need for hard and back-breaking human toil also made it possible for men as well as women to dispense with foods with high caloric contents: for, as became generally known, calories were required largely to supply heat and replace rapidly wearing out body tissue. 5. Cotton was being replaced by rayons and other chemically produced fabrics. 6. Finally, agriculture itself had become more efficient, making it possible to produce more foods and fibers for each dollar of labor and capital expended. In fact, between 1919 and 1929, on a stationary cultivated acreage, the output of American farmers increased more than 20 per cent. There were notably three reasons responsible for this revolutionary advance: progress in the application of mechanical methods and the motorization of farm equipment (with an accompanying decrease of land use necessary for the provision of feed grains for horses and mules); increasing acre yields as a result of intensive cultivation, the improvement of crop strains, and the application of fertilizer; and the greater efficiency of milk and meat animals per unit of feed consumed. There was, therefore, a surplus of farmers in the United States.

— Document No. 23 —

THE POSITION OF LABOR[23]

[23] Louis M. Hacker, *American Problems of Today* (New York, 1938), pp. 80 ff.

The inability of labor to expand its activities and the frustrations it encountered as a result of court action were characteristics of the 1920s. The following is from Louis M. Hacker's American Problems of Today.

✓   ✓   ✓

It was no accident, therefore, that the years in question were years of waning trade-union militancy. Class collaboration was the keynote of traditional trade unionism; and the unskilled were compelled to fend for themselves. One finds therefore that whereas membership in American trade unions grew fairly steadily until the end of the World War, it began thenceforth to decline. Industrial disputes also decreased in numbers and duration. In 1897, there had been 447,000 American trade unionists; in 1900, 868,500; by 1914, 2,716,900; and in 1920—the all time peak until 1937—5,110,800. By 1922, the trade unions had lost a million members; and in 1929 the total membership was 4,330,000. . . .

Some of the reasons for organized labor's inability to grow in the postwar years were the following: 1. The traditional policy of voluntarism, first laid down by Samuel Gompers, which held that labor's advance could be furthered only by its own economic power. Hence, organized labor continued unwilling to organize for political action or to demand the intervention of the state in such vital matters as those pertaining to wages, hours, and social insurance. 2. The adoption of a class-collaboration program. Voluntarism, on its other face, called for working-class militancy; and this the leadership of the American Federation of Labor eschewed. In the words of David J. Saposs, the keenest student of the problem of the period: ". . . union-management cooperation was elevated to a cardinal principle and was substituted for belligerency as the program of voluntarism. The new procedure was to sell unionism to the employer. If he recognized the union and permitted his workers to join it, the union in turn would cooperate in setting up machinery which would cooperate with the employer in increasing his profits through reducing costs and enlarging his markets. . . . The union now became a service agency equally interested not only in its own welfare but in that of the employer."

This program, however, was successful only with lesser employers; the great mass industries refused the proffered hand of friendship. 3. Mechanization, which was destroying rapidly the skills of the old-time artisans and hence rendering the old craft distinctions obsolete. With organized labor's refusal to shift from a craft to an industrial basis, its chances for winning over the country's great body of workers became increasingly slighter. 4. Welfare capitalism (that is to say, company health, recreational, and insurance programs), which sought to give the workers at least the same benefits as were offered by the conservative unions. 5. Open shop movements and company unions. 6. Yellow-dog contracts, as a result of which unions might be enjoined from organizing those individual workers who had signed such agreements with their employers. 7. The refusal on the part of most of the A.F. of L. unions to admit into their memberships Negro workers. 8. Labor injunctions, which placed serious obstacles in the path of unions engaged in industrial disputes. These last two phenomena we must examine at greater length.

In the fifteen years beginning with 1915, fully one million Negroes poured into the industrial centers of the North and West to work in West Virginia and Illinois coal mines, Chicago and Kansas City packing plants, Detroit automobile factories, Pittsburgh, Cleveland, and Joliet steel and iron mills. In considerable measure, the northern factory managers began by regarding the Negroes as an industrial reserve, who, because they had no class consciousness, could be used to break the strikes of the white craft unions. The Negro was not averse to strikebreaking for a number of reasons: In the first place, the wages, living conditions, and opportunities for leisure that the northern factory communities offered him were immeasurably superior to anything he had enjoyed in the South. Again, the Negro's slave heritage—strengthened in the period following the Civil War by the preachments of such leaders as Booker T. Washington, by the Negro churches, and by northern white philanthropy—made him regard the white worker as a natural foe and the white employer as a trusted friend and well-wisher. In the third place, the great majority of the Negroes coming from the cotton country were really completely unfamiliar with trade unionism and class solidarity, if not with factories themselves. Most significant of all was the failure of the craft unions to admit into their ranks these new industrial laborers. Openly or not, the policies of the international and national craft unions were based on exclusion. And from 1890 on the American Federation of Labor itself gave support to this attitude by refusing to bring pressure to bear on its constituent organizations and by seeking to unionize Negroes not as locals in the national unions but as weak federal locals under direct aegis of the Federation itself. The class conscious Negro worker "scabbed" because of his hatred for such tactics and because of his desire to pay back the white unionists in their own coin.

The chief weapon against organized labor, in the armory of capital, was not violence or counter-organization so much as the use of a peculiarly American legal device, that is to say, the injunction. Appealing to federal and state courts sitting in equity (on the ground that substantive law was deficient) employers in increasing numbers, beginning with the nineties, took to suing for injunctions to prevent labor unions and striking workers from committing irreparable injury to their property. The courts were quick to grant the type of relief requested. Also, the process was a swift and a successful one. During the nineteen twenties, the most common forms of injunctions, sued for against workers and their representatives the trade unions, were the following: from engaging in strikes (whether local, general, or sympathetic); from assembling to act or organize for a strike; from paying strike benefits; from engaging in boycotts; from picketing; from adopting rules against the handling of goods made by nonunion labor; from making trade agreements with employers stipulating the employment of union labor only and the production of goods under union conditions; from making trade agreements for the limitation of production; from sabotaging and the use of violence. . . .

— Document No. 24 —

ROOSEVELT'S NEW DEAL[24]

Franklin D. Roosevelt was convinced that heroic measures were necessary if Americans were to be restored to their faith in capitalist institutions. He sought to personalize the errors and failures of the 1920s; to this extent he was making political, or politicians' judgments; but his confidence was impressive, and it helped greatly during the dark years of the early 1930s. The first document is from an address he delivered at the Commonwealth Club in San Francisco during the Presidential campaign, September, 1932; the second is from his First Inaugural Address.

✓   ✓   ✓

I

A glance at the situation today only too clearly indicates that equality of opportunity as we have known it no longer exists. Our industrial plant is built; the problem just now is whether under existing conditions it is not overbuilt. Our last frontier has long since been reached, and there is practically no more free land. More than half of our people do not live on the farms or on lands and cannot derive a living by cultivating their own property. There is no safety valve in the form of a western prairie to which those thrown out of work by the Eastern economic machines can go for a new start. We are not able to invite the immigration from Europe to share our endless plenty. We are now providing a drab loving for our own people. . . .

Clearly, all this calls for a re-appraisal of values. A mere builder of more industrial plants, a creator of more railroad systems, an organizer of more corporations, is

[24] From contemporary newspapers.

as likely to be a danger as a help. The day of the great promoter of the financial Titan, to whom we granted anything if only he would build, or develop, is over. Our task now is not discovery or exploitation of natural resources, or necessarily producing more goods. It is the soberer, less dramatic business of administering resources and plants already in hand, of seeking to reestablish foreign markets for our surplus production, of meeting the problem of underconsumption, of adjusting production to consumption, of distributing wealth and products more equitably, of adapting existing economic organizations to the service of the people. The day of enlightened administration has come. . . .

As I see it, the task of Government in its relation to business is to assist the development of an economic declaration of rights, an economic constitutional order. This is the common task of statesman and business man. It is the minimum requirement of a more permanently safe order of things.

Happily, the times indicate that to create such an order not only is the proper policy of Government, but it is the only line of safety for our economic structures as well. We know, now, that these economic units cannot exist unless prosperity is uniform, that is, unless purchasing power is well distributed throughout every group in the Nation. That is why even the most selfish of corporations for its own interest would be glad to see wages restored and unemployment ended and to bring the Western farmer back to his accustomed level of prosperity and to assure a permanent safety to both groups. That is why some enlightened industries themselves endeavor to limit the freedom of action of each man and business group within the industry in the common interest of all; why business men everywhere are asking a form of organization which will bring the scheme of things into balance, even though it may in some measure qualify the freedom of action of individual units within the business. . . .

II

I am certain that my fellow Americans expect that on my induction into the Presidency I will address them with a candor and a decision which the present situation of our

Nation impels. This is preeminently the time to speak the truth, the whole truth, frankly and boldly. Nor need we shrink from honestly facing conditions in our country today. This great Nation will endure as it has endured, will revive and will prosper. So, first of all, let me assert my firm belief that the only thing we have to fear is fear itself—nameless, unreasoning, unjustified terror which paralyzes needed efforts to convert retreat into advance. In every dark hour of our national life a leadership of frankness and vigor has met with that understanding and support of the people themselves which is essential to victory. I am convinced that you will again give that support to leadership in these critical days.

In such a spirit on my part and on yours we face our common difficulties. They concern, thank God, only material things. Values have shrunken to fantastic levels; taxes have risen; our ability to pay has fallen; government of all kinds is faced by serious curtailment of income; the means of exchange are frozen in the currents of trade; the withered leaves of industrial enterprise lie on every side; farmers find no markets for their produce; the savings of many years in thousands of families are gone.

More important, a host of unemployed citizens face the grim problem of existence, and an equally great number toil with little return. Only a foolish optimist can deny the dark realities of the moment.

Yet our distress comes from no failure of substance. . . . Plenty is at our doorstep, but a generous use of it languishes in the very sight of the supply. Primarily this is because rulers of the exchange of mankind's goods have failed through their own stubbornness and their own incompetence, have admitted their failure, and have abdicated. Practices of the unscrupulous money changers stand indicted in the court of public opinion, rejected by the hearts and minds of men. . . .

The money changers have fled from their high seats in the temple of our civilization. We may now restore that temple to the ancient truths. The measure of the restoration lies in the extent to which we apply social values more noble than mere monetary profit. . . .

Restoration calls, however, not for changes in ethics alone. . . .

Our greatest primary task is to put people to work.

This is no unsolvable problem if we face it wisely and courageously. It can be accomplished in part by direct recruiting by the Government itself, treating the task as we would treat the emergency of a war. . . .

Finally, in our progress toward a resumption of work we require two safeguards against a return of the evils of the old order: there must be a strict supervision of all banking and credits and investments, so that there will be an end to speculation with other people's money and there must be provision for an adequate but sound currency. . . .

Through this program of action we address ourselves to putting our own national house in order and making income balance outgo. Our international trade relations, though vastly important, are in point of time and necessity secondary to the establishment of a sound national economy. I shall spare no effort to restore world trade by international economic readjustment, but the emergency at home cannot wait on that accomplishment. . . .

In the field of world policy I would dedicate this Nation to the policy of the good neighbor—the neighbor who resolutely respects himself and, because he does so, respects the rights of others—the neighbor who respects his obligations and respects the sanctity of his agreements in and with a world of neighbors.

If I read the temper of our people correctly, we now realize as we have never realized before our interdependence on each other; that we cannot merely take but we must give as well; that if we are to go forward, we must move as a trained and loyal army willing to sacrifice for the good of a common discipline, because without such discipline no progress is made, no leadership becomes effective. We are, I know, ready and willing to submit our lives and property to such discipline, because it makes possible a leadership which aims at a larger good. This I propose to offer, pledging that the larger purposes will bind upon us all as a sacred obligation with a unity of duty hitherto evoked only in time of armed strife. . . .

— Document No. 25 —

THE REASONS FOR GOVERNMENT INTERVENTION [25]

New Deal economists were convinced that traditional mechanisms in the economy had broken down and massive intervention on the part of the federal government was imperative. The following document is a characteristic statement; it was the work of Gardner C. Means, an administration economist, and was presented in 1935.

✔   ✔   ✔

PART I. THE BASIC CAUSE FOR THE FAILURE OF A LAISSEZ FAIRE POLICY

1. The National Recovery Administration and Agricultural Adjustment Administration were created in response to an overwhelming demand from many quarters that certain elements in the making of industrial policy (including agriculture as an industry) should no longer be left to the market place and the price mechanism but should be placed in the hands of administrative bodies— code authorities, crop control committees, etc. . . .

2. The whole trend of social development both in this country and abroad has been to recognize the failure of a complete laissez faire policy.

3. The basic cause for the failure of a laissez faire policy is to be found in the very same forces which have made possible a high standard of living for all, namely, the gradual, century-long shift from market to administrative coordination of economic activity which has resulted in modern industrial organization and modern technology. This shift to administration has brought a

[25] "Industrial Prices and their Relative Inflexibility," Senate Document No. 13, 74th Congr., 1st Sess. (Washington, 1935.)

new type of competition and inflexible administered prices which disrupt the workings of the market.

4. A century ago the great bulk of economic activity in the United States was conducted on an atomistic basis by individuals or families—as is most of agriculture today—while the actions of the separate individuals were coordinated by the market. The individual produced for sale and his activity was geared to and in part controlled by flexible market prices. . . .

5. But gradually more and more of economic coordination has been accomplished administratively. Great numbers of individuals have been drawn into large factories or business organizations and their activities have come to be coordinated within the separate enterprises by administrative action. . . . In 1929 the activity of over 400,000 workers was meshed into a great communication system by the management of the American Telephone & Telegraph Co. Contrast the coordination and balance among this group of workers with that among 400,000 separate farmers whose action in producing more or less of each product is controlled and balanced only by the market. . . .

6. The shift from market to administrative coordination has gone so far that a major part of American economic activity is now carried on by great administrative units—our great corporations. More than half of all manufacturing activity is carried on by 200 big corporations. . . .

7. This development of administrative coordination has made possible tremendous increases in the efficiency of industrial production within single enterprises. The large number of workers brought into a single organization has allowed a high degree of subdivision of labor and the use of complicated series of machines so that the volume of production has been expanded way beyond the capacity of the same number of workers operating independently. . . .

8. But the very concentration of economic activity which brought increased productivity has by its nature destroyed the free market and disrupted the operations of the law of supply and demand in a great many industries and for the economy as a whole.

9. Evidence of this disruption is to be found in the

administrative character and relative inflexibility of price in a great many industries and the fact that on the whole prices during the depression have tended to go down least where the drop in demand has been greatest.

10. The failure of prices to adjust is perfectly familiar to business men in nearly every industry. But the implications of this familiar fact for the economy as a whole have not been recognized.

11. In a large part of industry, the market is not equating supply and demand through a flexible price mechanism, but is bringing an adjustment of production to demand at administratively determined prices. . . .

12. The presence of administered prices, while it does not indicate monopoly, does mean that the number of concerns competing in the market has been reduced to the point that the individual concern has a significant power to choose within limits between changing its prices and changing its volume of production or sales. . . .

13. But this means that individuals have a direct power over industrial policy which they exercise in making business policy for their own enterprise.

14. The distinction drawn here between industrial policy and business policy is of the greatest importance.

15. According to laissez faire principles, industrial policy was supposed to result from the interaction in the market of the business policies of a large number of independent units, no one of which had any significant power. In the truly atomistic economy to which the principles of laissez faire applied, no individual buyer or seller alone had any significant power over either price or total volume of production for the industry. . . .

16. Where the number of competing units in a particular industry have been reduced to a relatively small handful, industrial policy is no longer made wholly by the market but in part by individuals. . . .

17. But when the business man has the power to affect industrial policy, he almost necessarily makes wrong industrial decisions. The very position, experience and training of the business man which lead him to make the correct decisions on business policy tend to force him to make the wrong decisions on industrial policy in spite

of the utmost public spirit which he, as an individual, may seek to exercise. . . .

18. The business man is expected to make business policy in a way to maximize the profits of his own enterprise. When he has the power to choose between lowering price and lowering production, good business policy frequently requires him in the presence of falling demand to hold price and curtail his production even though this means idle hands and idle machines. . . . His interest dictates lowering price only when he is able to squeeze his costs, particularly his labor costs. . . . It is only because this holding of prices has become widespread and customary that the term "price chiseler" could be a term of opprobrium in an economy supposed to be coordinated through flexible prices.

19. The net effect of business control over industrial policy is, therefore, to aggravate any fluctuations in economic activity and prevent any necessary readjustments. An initial drop in demand would result, not in price readjustment, but in maintained prices and curtailment of production, thus throwing workers and machines out of employment, reducing money income and spending power, and further reducing demand. The inflexible administered prices resulting from the shift from market to administration thus act as a disrupting factor in the economy and could cause an initial small drop in demand to become a national disaster. . . .

— Document No. 26 —

THE NEW DEAL'S FISCAL POLICIES [26]

While the New Deal moved virtually into every area of the economy—to regulate and control, buy and spend— it understood that a major tool for restarting the economic engine was through monetary and fiscal devices. The two statements that follow are an historian's summary and a declaration by a contemporary policymaker. The first document is from Louis M. Hacker's The Shaping of the American Tradition *and the second from an address delivered by Marriner S. Eccles, at that time (1939) Chairman of the Board of Governors of the Federal Reserve System. It is apparent that, as late as 1939, public officials at Washington still could see heavy government spending as the only real way of getting the economy back on its feet.*

I

Roosevelt's First Inaugural had pledged reform of the banking system, a promise fulfilled in August, 1935, when the President signed the Banking Act of that year. This provided for increased government control of the Federal Reserve System: the President was not only to appoint all members of its Board of Governors—who were to approve the person chosen to be president of each Federal Reserve Bank—but the Board of Governors was to con-

---

[26] Louis M. Hacker, *The Shaping of the American Tradition,* 2 vols. (New York, 1947), pp. 1195-97; R. L. Weissman, ed. *Economic Balance and a Balanced Budget* (New York, 1940). Reprinted by permission of Harper and Brothers.

trol the Open Market Committee, which had power over the expansion and contraction of bank credits. The Board of Governors was also given the right to raise the reserve requirements of member banks to double the existing maximums, a measure which could prevent the additional currency authorized by acts of Congress from inflating the economy. In addition, the act allowed reserve banks to make loans to their members on time or demand notes of four months' maturity and national banks were given the right to make loans on real estate, which allowed competition with state banks that had such power. But national banks were forbidden to participate in the underwriting of security issues. At the 1935 meeting of the American Bankers' Association, Marriner S. Eccles (1890-   ), one of the governors of the Federal Reserve Board and soon to become chairman of the renamed Board of Governors of the Federal Reserve System, explained the purposes of the new law and urged the banking community to give its cooperation.

Government intervention in the nation's financial activities has been necessary to save the country from its "state of disastrous contraction." The RFC has helped the nation's banks. The Home Owners' Loan Corporation had relieved both banks and the harassed homeowner, thus benefiting creditors as well as debtors. The Federal Farm Mortgage Corporation has prevented the collapse of the farm mortgage market by providing funds, through the issue of government bonds, to be loaned to Federal Land Banks in return for their own mortgage-backed bonds. The services of these agencies and of the relief program have been worth their cost despite the unbalancing of the budget, Eccles argues. For taxes and government debt are not to be considered as mathematical absolutes but in relation to national income. Hence, while a deficit may not be desirable, it is not necessarily destructive. In the present situation, bankers must be ready to extend credit in the form their communities require rather than according to the precepts of liquidity. Eccles then turns from a defense of the administration's policy of what may be called financial "relief" to a defense of government intervention to prevent deflation. When such tendencies appear, government should not decrease spending, for that promotes further deflation, the collapse of confidence, and depression.

II

We may say then I think, that our greatest domestic problem—the major task before the nation—is to find productive employment for all of our people capable of working who are now unable to find employment. The magnitude of the problem is measured by the number of these people. Allowing for a certain unavoidable minimum of unemployment due to seasonal and other special reasons, there are more than eight million men and women for whom work should be found.

That it is not a scarcity of money that prevents a more satisfactory economic condition from developing is clear from the fact that our supply of money represented by demand deposits and currency today is larger by several billions of dollars and interest rates are lower than ever before in our history. In addition, the excess reserves of member banks at the present time exceed $4 billions, a heretofore undreamed of surplus. These reserves could become the basis for a further expansion of our money supply to the extent of more than $25 billions. . . .

We hear it said continually that there is an absence of risk or venture capital willing to go into new enterprise. I do not think there is an absence of the capital, but there undoubtedly is an unwillingness to assume the risk. I think that this may be due in part, but only in relatively small part, to the fact that the entrepreneur who is in the upper income brackets feels that he is as well off buying money in some new business. I am convinced, however, that if markets existed for additional products of existing enterprise, or if new markets were in sight calling for additions to existing enterprise, or if new inventions were at hand for which a demand would probably develop, there would be no lack of risk capital willing to undertake the necessary investment. . . .

As we look about us today, the most promising fields in which to put idle men, money and materials to work are housing, railroad, and to a lesser degree, the utilities. These are the fields in which the depression struck deepest and the unemployment was greatest. I believe we could do much in all three fields. . . .

But when we add up all the amounts we could possibly hope to expend under the most favorable conditions in these three fields of private housing, railroads and electric power, we come out with the figure of between $5 and $6 billions, which is small in relation to the magnitude of funds that have to find outlets for investment under the present distribution of the national income if we are to achieve full employment.

With the slower tempo of our national growth, and being now a creditor and not a debtor nation in need of capital, we must devise means to enlarge the domestic market for our products. To do this we need a better balanced distribution of our national income, which in turn involves the steady channeling of additional funds into the hands of those at the lower end of our income scale. . . .

Perhaps the most important single step that can be taken now to increase the purchasing power of consumers and thus to diminish the need for investment outlets is to revamp our present old-age insurance program. Under this plan by the end of this year it is estimated that there will have been collected from payroll taxes $1.7 billions, this burden falling almost entirely on consumers, whereas, practically nothing has been paid out in benefits. It is so constructed as to collect taxes from young men now with a view to taking care of them when they become old. This system needs to be so revised as to provide a reasonable pension to old people immediately, regardless of whether or not they have contributed to the fund. This would not only meet a great social need and popular demand, but would also be a sound economic measure at this stage in our economic life.

The present plan is operating as a gigantic saving device at a time when there is a surfeit of saving; it is decreasing consumption when we have inadequate consumer buying power. It would be appropriate to a capital-poor country where a curtailment of consumption was necessary in order to divert more resources into the making of plant and equipment. It has no possible economic justification, however, in our capital-rich, consumption-poor economy. . . .

In order to provide for the maximum possible elasticity in our economy so that there will be no obstructions to

the income flow, we must find means of controlling mo-
nopolistic and other uneconomic practices both by industry and by labor.

The policies of many of our large industries to meet
a decline in demand by radical curtailment of output,
while leaving prices at high levels, result in accentuating
depressions. On the other hand, rapid price advances at
the first indications of the return of a lively demand tend
to bring an upswing in business to an end. These policies
tend to create maladjustment between industrial and
agricultural prices, which in turn have a seriously disturbing effect on the whole economy. Better planning of production and price policies by business concerns with
reference to more than the short-time garnering of profits
would do much to reduce violent fluctuations in business. . . .

I have given much thought and study to the analysis
which I have presented to you. I come out with the firm
conviction that, in order to keep up the flow of income
and prevent the progress of our economy from being
arrested, we must adopt—in addition to the various measures and proposals that I have outlined—a program, on
the one hand, of increasing consumption relative to the
national income through the development of old-age pen-
sions, health and other social services and, on the other
hand, of undertaking increased public investment in useful
enterprises of a kind that private capital will not undertake, but which, nevertheless, can be in large part self-
liquidating. Such public investment could take the form
of toll roads, tunnels and bridges; rural rehabilitation and
farm tenancy loans, especially in the south, to make our
farmers independent and self-supporting; and an extension of the rural electrification program; hospital and san-
itation facilities to reduce the appalling economic waste
of sickness and to make our people healthier and more
efficient; and expansion of public housing for the lowest
income groups. . . .

— Document No. 27 —

PRODUCTIVITY AND ECONOMIC PROGRESS [27]

Frederick C. Mills, distinguished American econo- mist and statistician, seeks to measure the economic growth of the United States during the half-century 1901- 50. He comes to the conclusion that there has been im- pressive economic progress—indicated notably in rising per capita consumption—as a result of improved pro- ductivity.

✓   ✓   ✓

Over the last half century the real national product of the United States increased five-fold, while population doubled. Output per capita of the population increased two and one-half times. Here was the basis of a substan- tial advance in economic power and in levels of consump- tion. Over this same period the total volume of human effort going into production (measured by manhours of labor input) increased by 80 per cent. The great gain in total output was won with an increase in labor input well below the increase in population. Here is evidence of a gain in welfare in another dimension—a saving of effort and a lightening of the toil by which the material needs of life are satisfied.

The major instrument used in the winning of these dual gains was enhanced productivity. During this period there was an unbroken advance in average physical output per manhour of work done. Decade by decade the effective- ness of productive effort increased. In the final decade output per manhour of labor input was 2.81 times what it was fifty years before. . . .

[27] Frederick C. Mills, "Productivity and Economic Progress," Occasional Paper 38 (New York, 1952). Reprinted by permission of National Bureau of Economic Research, Inc.

The chief lifting force between the first and the fifth decades was steadily growing productivity. This increment grew from 76 billions (of 1929 dollars) in 1901-10 to 212 billions in 1921-30. Relatively, this last was the greatest productivity gain of the half century. There was a drop in the depressed thirties, but even in that decade the productivity increment was more than large enough to offset the loss of 141 billions resulting from a great decline in the volume of labor input. The most recent decade brought a productivity increment of 213 billion dollars, a figure approximately equal to the gain of the twenties. The employed labor force in the latest decade was the largest in our history and this, of course, served to enhance the gain resulting from the actual advance in manhour productivity. Great as it was, the productivity increment in this decade was materially exceeded by the labor input increment. Additions to manpower, supplemented by increases in output per manhour, gave us the tremendous increment to product upon which we drew for guns and butter in the forties.

I have said that the relative gains in productivity were greatest in the twenties. To the student of economic growth, indeed, special interest attaches to the period of six or eight years following the end of the first world war. In these years rates of acceleration in manhour productivity in the economy at large and in the important manufacturing sector reached their maxima, for the fifty-year period here reviewed. For the whole economy the rate of productivity gain attained almost 4 per cent a year between 1918 and 1924. In manufacturing industries output per manhour increased at a rate of 10 per cent a year for each of the three years between 1919 and 1922, an advance probably without precedent in our industrial history.

Back of these advances lay a highly favorable conjuncture of circumstances. The movement toward scientific management came to first fruition in the industrial expansion of the early twenties. The moving assembly line, dramatized by Ford a few years earlier, became a standard feature of mass production. The power available to industrial workers was greatly increased in amount and in flexibility of application. Working hours declined from 53 a week in 1914 and 1917 to an average of 47 in 1922.

Occupational shifts contributed to the gain in manhour output in the general economy. In the recovery that followed the readjustment after World War I the number of persons in the relatively highly paid tertiary occupations grew, while employment in agriculture and in manufacturing lagged, or declined. The stock of real capital per worker, in the form of producers' durable equipment and industrial and commercial structures, stood at a relatively high level in the early twenties, having increased by some 40 per cent in two decades. No comparable rise occurred until the notable increase that followed the end of World War II. Perhaps of greater importance than the increase in the stock of capital goods was the advance in the *quality* of capital instruments. Technological improvements as well as the innovations of scientific management were widely adopted in the early twenties; such improvements were chiefly manifest in the tools of production. These diverse factors combined with others in the complex of working conditions that determine productive effectiveness to yield a remarkable productivity gain. . . .

We obtain a clearer view of the historical course of consumption levels by reducing the consumption increments to per capita terms, and showing each decade gain against the pre-existing level of per capita consumption. This is done in the following table; the expenditure figures are decade totals, per capita.

Decade	Per capita consumer expenditures (1929 dollars)	Change from preceding decade Absolute (1929 dollars)	Relative (per cent)
1891-1900	3,157		
1901-10	4,166	1,009	+32
1911-20	4,537	371	+9
1921-30	5,741	1,204	+27
1931-40	5,670	71	−1
1941-50	7,692	2,022	+36

In the preceding pages we have discussed the pattern of economic growth of the United States over the last half century. The materials presented bear on questions central to the appraisal of an economic system. Has it produced? Has it grown in effectiveness as a producing

mechanism? It was Ernest Bevin's view that the central
test of an economy is "Has it delivered the goods?" But
this cannot be the sole criterion of judgment. We must
ask "How has productive power been used?" This question raises issues beyond the economic. Arnold Toynbee
has said that the new power found through the simplifica-
tion of process that generates the growth of civilizations
always presents a moral challenge. Disposable resources
may be used to promote welfare or illfare. In a progressive economy, marked by steadily recurring productivity
increments and expanding margins above maintenance
needs, each generation faces this challenge anew.

Our economy, in its performance over the first half
of the twentieth century, has clearly met Bevin's test.
We have used our natural resources to produce a great
and growing volume of goods and services. Apart from
the protracted check that came in the thirties, the advance has been virtually unbroken. By far the greatest
factor in this gain has been rising productivity. Machines,
plants, administrative methods, and men have improved
in productive quality; equipment has grown in quantity;
flexible power has been carried to assembly line and
bench. These improvements, embodied in innumerable
major and minor working methods, have brought an increase in output per unit of productive effort that is
probably without precedent in our history. . . .

— Document No. 28 —

THE ACCOMPLISHMENTS OF THE 1950s [28]

*The high prosperity of the United States during the
1950s received careful (and perhaps prayerful) attention
from Americans. It was being assumed that the base for*

[28] "Economic Report of the President." Transmitted to the
Congress, January 24, 1956.

prosperity was broader than it had been in the 1920s; in the second place, government intervention was accepted as normal. In 1946, the Employment Act called for a periodical examination of the economy by a so-called Council of Economic Advisers to the President. The document that follows emanates from that body and was, presumably, written by its Chairman, Arthur F. Burns, Columbia University Professor of Economics.

✓   ✓   ✓

I. NEW LEVELS OF ECONOMIC ACTIVITY

Our economy has broken through to new and higher ground. . . . We have reached the threshold of a 400 billion dollar economy, and the recent advance has been accomplished without the specious aid of price inflation.

The rapidity of recent progress is seen most clearly in aggregate measures of economic activity that allow for seasonal variations. The most comprehensive of these measures is the gross national product—that is, the dollar value of the Nation's output of commodities and services. . . . At present it is 397 billion, if not higher. . . .

Another comprehensive measure of economic activity is civilian employment—that is, the number of men and women, outside the Armed Forces, who work in their own businesses or are employed by others. At the peak of the economic expansion which culminated in July 1953, about 62.5 million men and women were at work. A year later, employment was reduced to 61 million. Since then employment has risen rather steadily, passing the 62 million mark in April 1955 and reaching 64.6 million in December. . . .

Still another comprehensive measure of economic activity is the amount of income disbursed to people by private industry and government. In the second quarter of 1953, incomes were flowing to individuals at an annual rate of slightly over 290 billion dollars. . . . The recent expansion has brought income disbursements to an annual rate of 318 billion dollars. This increase in dollar income during the past two years has constituted a genuine addition to buying power, since average prices in consumer markets have been virtually steady while taxes have been lower. . . .

With incomes generally improving, the spending of people has mounted. Consumer expenditures, counting investments in new homes besides ordinary outlays on consumption, increased from an annual rate of 248 billion dollars in the second quarter of 1954 to 274 billion in the final quarter of 1955. Consumers have benefited not only from the growth of the economy, but also from the extensive shift of resources to civilian uses that the close of hostilities in Korea and continued governmental economies made possible. While the annual rate of the Nation's total output has increased about 28 billion dollars since the spring of 1953, the rate of expenditure in the consumer sector has increased a full 30 billion. Thus, the physical resources and manpower released by the Federal Government have been used preponderantly in the production of homes, automobiles, television sets, and the thousand-and-one articles and services that flow directly to consumers and enrich the everyday lives of people. At the same time, the provision of new and improved tools of production, on which future advances in our living standards depend, has gone forward on an extensive scale. . . .

II. EXPANSION THROUGH FREE ENTERPRISE

Many factors have been quietly adding to the strength of our economy, and the current expansion is fundamentally an expression of their cumulating force. Among these factors are the unexpectedly large upsurge of population in the past decade, the continued growth of scientific knowledge, the onrush of technology, the rapid obsolescence of what is sometimes regarded as fixed capital, the recent development of long-range investment planning by industry, the improved control over inventories, the intensified pace of business competition, th' wide diffusion of well-being among people, their insistent and growing desire to earn more and live better, the development of mass markets to match mass production, the rebuilding of Western Europe, the general recognition of government's responsibility in helping to maintain a stable prosperity, and the growing understanding that public policy must protect economic incentives if enterprise, innovation, and investment are to flourish. All these factors are and probably will continue to be basic to our progress, but several of them are especially note-worthy in the current situation. . . .

The Federal Government has played a constructive part in the prosperity that the American people are now experiencing so widely. It has not, however, sought to maintain good times by expanding our already huge governmental outlays or by permitting the value of money to depreciate. Recognizing that these alluring short cuts to a high level of economic activity have all too often brought disaster to nations, our governmental policies have concentrated on building an economic environment that favors an orderly expansion of private activities.

The demands of modern life and the continuing threat of Communist aggression require a much higher level of taxes and a larger role of Government in economic affairs than suited earlier generations. This very fact imposes a responsibility on the Government to pursue policies that will help to keep the private economy strong and growing. The Administration has sought, in cooperation with the Congress, to discharge its responsibility through a series of closely related policies. First, by removing direct controls over prices and wages, which had outlived their usefulness. Second, by preserving an actively competitive environment and assisting new and small businesses. Third, by curtailing governmental activities that could be handled as well or better by private enterprise. Fourth, by restricting public expenditures, and yet adding to the country's defensive strength and its stock of public assets, especially highways, hospitals, and educational facilities. Fifth, by lightening the burden of taxes. . . . Seventh, by tempering the impact of unemployment, old age, illness, and blighted neighborhoods on people, yet not impairing self-reliance. Eighth, by extending the automatic workings of our fiscal system that tend to offset or cushion changes in income arising from changes in economic activity. Ninth, by attacking fundamental causes of weakness in the farm situation. Tenth, by acting promptly and resolutely when either recessionary or inflationary influences in the general economy became evident.

By recognizing the vital importance in our times both of free enterprise and of a sense of economic security, these directions of governmental policy have served to enlarge the horizons of businessmen, workers, investors and consumers, and have stimulated people to bolder economic actions and undertakings. This, in essence, has been the Government's role in the recent expansion. . . .

— Document No. 29 —

THE FINANCIAL POSITION OF CONSUMERS [29]

Government agencies followed closely the position of consumers in the economy, for they were aware of the vital role consumer power plays. The document that follows is from the monthly "Federal Reserve Bulletin," June, 1956.

The year 1955 was a period of expanding business activity and increasing consumer incomes and expenditures. According to Department of Commerce estimates, aggregate personal income was $16 billion larger in 1955 than in 1954. Data from the 1956 Survey of Consumer Finances point to a wide distribution of the increase among consumer spending units.

Expansion of consumer expenditures, including those for houses and consumer durable goods, was accompanied by rising mortgage and short-term indebtedness. Consumer holdings of liquid assets also increased despite the high level of consumer spending and large acquisitions of nonliquid assets. . . .

INCOME. The increase in consumer income in 1955

[29] Board of Governors of the Federal Reserve System, "Federal Reserve Bulletin," June, 1956 (Washington, 1956), pp. 559-67.

was apparently spread over most of the income scale. According to Survey of Consumer Finances data, the median income of all spending units—that is, the income of the middlemost unit—rose from $3,700 in 1954 to $3,960 in 1955, or about 7 per cent. Mean reported income—that is, the figure obtained by dividing total reported income by the number of spending units—rose from $4,420 to $4,650, or about 5 per cent. Survey income data include only money income, and certain groups of spending units, including transients and residents of institutions, are excluded from the sample. Moreover, the Survey probably does not account adequately for the very large incomes, which are of particular importance for the mean.

About 36 per cent of all spending units reported incomes of $4,000 or more in 1955 compared with 32 per cent in the preceding year. The proportion with incomes from $2,000 to $5,000 declined from 45 to 41 per cent while the proportion with incomes below $2,000 remained unchanged at about 23 per cent. The lowest income groups include many persons who are retired or who for other reasons are not working full time and whose incomes are not particularly responsive to many forces that tend to increase the higher incomes. Moreover, it is probable that Survey data conceal some rise in the level of incomes in the lower brackets. . . .

The growth of income in 1955 continued the upward trend that has prevailed with only brief interruptions since the war. From 1947 to 1955 median money income rose 57 per cent, and the proportion of persons earning $5,000 or more increased about one and one-half times. The rise in incomes was offset only in part by a 20 per cent rise in consumer prices, as measured by the Bureau of Labor Statistics index. The proportion of spending units receiving the equivalent of $5,000 or more in 1955 dollars increased about two-thirds from 1947 to 1955. . . .

— Document No. 30 —

THE MODERN CORPORATION[30]

During the 1950s, Americans were beginning to shake off some of those dreads of "bigness" that had guided so much public policy in the 1900s and the 1930s. Adolf A. Berle, Jr., asked for a new view of corporate power in his The 20th Century Capitalist Revolution. *He had been an official of the New Deal in the 1930s and 1940s; it is apparent, however, in the selection below, that he is ready to re-examine some of the preconceptions that shaped the attitudes of America twenty years earlier. The selection is from Chapter II of his book and is called* Corporate Power and Modern Capitalism.

✓   ✓   ✓

The two most notable achievements of the twentieth century corporations have been their ability to concentrate economic power in themselves and their ability to increase production and distribution. Apparently the power is essential to the productivity though that relationship is not definitively established. Actually they do go together, which is all we need to know for the moment.

The extent of the concentration of power may be very briefly stated, since our real interest is in the politics rather than the economics of the situation. According to a most careful and wholly unbiased estimate—that of Professor M. A. Adelman of Massachusetts Institute of Technology—135 corporations own 45 per cent of the industrial assets of the United States—or nearly one-fourth of the manufacturing volume of the entire world. . . .

[30] Adolf A. Berle, Jr., *The 20th Century Capitalist Revolution* (New York, 1954). Reprinted by permission of Harcourt, Brace and Company.

We cannot, however, leave the quantitative estimate quite there. Large corporations, in and of themselves, are impressive vehicles of power. Not less interesting is the fact that in a considerable and growing number of industries (covering an estimate 70 per cent of all American industry) a pattern has emerged—that which we may christen the "concentrate." American law, if not American economics, has in general prevented monopoly. But it has sanctioned and perhaps even encouraged a system, industry by industry, in which a few large corporations dominate the trade. Two or three, or at most, five corporations will have more than half the business, the remainder being divided among a greater or less number of smaller concerns who must necessarily live within the conditions made for them by the "Big Two" or "Big Three" or "Big Five" as the case may be. . . .

We are not excused, however, from looking beyond the simple arithmetic of property actually owned by corporations. The impact of many corporations—for example, General Motors or the great oil companies—goes beyond the confines of their actual ownership. For example, at a rough estimate, some three billions of dollars are invested in garages and facilities owned by so-called "small" businessmen who hold agency contracts from the principal automobile manufacturers. The owners are small, independent businessmen usually trading as "corporations" but certainly not giants. They are, nominally, independent. But their policies, operations, and, in large measure, their prices, are determined by the motor company whose cars they sell. The same is true of the "small businessman" who "owns" a gasoline-filling station. . . .

In any case, the aggregate result is hardly open to dispute. The mid-twentieth-century American capitalist system depends on and revolves around the operations of a relatively few very large corporations. It pivots upon industries most of which are concentrated in the hands of extremely few corporate units. Materially, the community has profited mightily. The system of large-scale production and mass distribution carried on by means of these large institutions can fairly claim the greatest share of credit. The face of the country has been changed. Poverty, in the sense that it is under-stood elsewhere in the world, in America is reduced to minimal proportions. Professor Louis Hacker of Columbia not unjustifiably calls it the "triumph of American capitalism." . . .

In November 1953, the economists for the National City Bank made an excellent brief study of the use and sources of capital. They calculated that in eight years (1946 to 1953 inclusive) an aggregate of 150 billions of dollars had been spent in the United States for capital expenditures, namely, modernizing and enlarging plant and equipment. This was spent by all of American business (excluding, of course, financial corporations like banks and insurance companies which deal not in physical assets but in money, credit, or evidence of debt of one kind or another). The figure is not surprising: the increase in American industrial plant was enormous and huge amounts of capital were needed. The spectacular fact is the source of this huge amount.

Sixty-four per cent of the 150 billion came from "internal sources," that is to say, receipts of the enterprises which had been accumulated and not distributed as dividends. Included in his figure (about 99 billion) were (1) retained earnings and (2) reserves set aside for depreciation, depletion, and amortization on past debt. Retained earnings were, of course, far and away the largest proportion.

Of the remaining 51 billion, or 36 per cent of the total, one-half was raised by current borrowing, chiefly represented (directly or indirectly) by bank credit. This accounts for approximately 25½ billion.

Eighteen billion, or 12 per cent of the total, was raised by issue of bonds or notes. This may fairly be said to have run the gauntlet of "market-place judgment," though the impact of it was changed and perhaps somewhat restricted by the fact that probably half of this amount was "privately placed." A private placement means that the enterprise does not offer bonds or securities for general subscription or purchase to the public; it negotiates with a large institution such as an insurance company or perhaps a syndicate of several such companies which buy all the issue.

Six per cent, or 9 billion, out of the total of 150 billion was raised by issue of stock. Here, and here only, do we begin to approach the "risk capital" investment so much relied on by classic economic theory. Even here a considerable amount was as far removed from "risk" as the situation permitted: without exact figures, apparently a majority of the 9 billion was represented by preferred stock. Probably not more than 5 billion of the total amount was represented by common stock—the one situation in which an investor considers an enterprise, decides on its probable usefulness and profitability, and puts down his savings, aware of a degree of risk but hoping for large profit.

There is substantial evidence, which need not be reviewed here, that this is representative of the real pattern of the twentieth-century capitalism. The capital is there; and so is capitalism. The waning factor is the capitalist. . . .

There are, undoubtedly, powerful exceptions to this trend. Utility companies, both in old industries such as telephone and electric light and power, and in new, such as those in the natural gas business, still seek and get large amounts of capital through the market place. But the number of enterprises, and the amount of capital they seek, has proportionably diminished. For practical purposes, the judgment of the market place in relation to application of capital has little application in the greatest and most dynamic areas of American industry.

Let us put this development into the context of our central problem of corporate power. The brief review above given even without other evidence which is available fairly justifies the conclusion that one of the classic checks on corporate power has been weakened, where it has not been removed altogether. A corporation like General Electric or General Motors which steadily builds its own capital, does not need to submit itself and its operations to the judgment of the financial markets. Power assumed to be brought under the review of banking and investment opinion a generation ago is now reviewed and checked chiefly by the conscience of its directors and managers.

BIBLIOGRAPHY

Berle, A. A., Jr. and Means, G., *Modern Corporation and Private Property* (New York, 1932).

Black, John P., *Agricultural Reform in the United States* (New York, 1929).

Clark, V. S., *History of Manufactures in the United States*, 3 vols. (New York, 1929).

Commons, John R. and associates, *History of Labour in the United States*, 4 vols. (New York, 1918-35).

Dewey, Davis R., *Financial History of the United States*, 12 ed. (New York, 1934).

Dewhurst, J. Frederic and associates, *America's Needs and Resources. A New Survey.* (New York, 1955).

Dorfman, Joseph, *The Economic Mind in American Civilization*, 3 vols. (New York, 1946-49).

Drucker, Peter F., *The New Society* (New York, 1949).

Dunbar, S. A., *History of Travel in America*, 4 vols. (Indianapolis, 1915).

Faulkner, Harold U., *The Decline of Laissez Faire, 1897-1917.* (New York, 1951).

Galbraith, G. K., *American Capitalism. The Concept of Countervailing Power* (Boston, 1952).

Gras, N. S. B. and Larson, Henrietta M., *Casebook in American Business History* (New York, 1939).

Gray, L. C., *History of Agriculture in the Southern United States to 1860*, 2 vols. (Washington, 1933).

Hacker, Louis M., *Alexander Hamilton in the American Tradition* (New York, 1957).

Hacker, Louis M., *Shaping of the American Tradition*, 2 vols. (New York, 1947).

Hacker, Louis M., *Triumph of American Capitalism* (New York, 1940).

Hansen, M. L., *The Immigrant in American History* (Cambridge, 1941).

Hutchins, J. G. B., *The American Maritime Industries and Public Policy. . . .* (Cambridge, 1941).

Kaempffert, W. B., ed., *Popular History of American Inventions*, 2 vols. (New York, 1924).

Kirkland, Edward C., *Men, Cities and Transportation*, 2 vols. (Cambridge, 1948).

Lambie, J. T. and Clemence, R. V., eds., *Economic Change in America* (Harrisburg, Pa., 1954).

Lewis, Cleona, *America's Stake in International Investments* (Washington, 1938).

Mitchell, Broadus, *Depression Decade . . . 1929-1941*. (New York, 1947).

Myers, Gustavus, *History of the Great American Fortunes* (New York, 1936).

Myers, Margaret G., *The New York Money Market*, 4 vols. (New York, 1931-32).

Pelzer, Louis, *The Cattleman's Frontier* (Glendale, Calif., 1936).

Ratner, Sidney, *American Taxation* (New York, 1942).

Shannon, Fred A., *The Farmer's Last Frontier. Agriculture, 1860-1897*. (New York, 1945).

Snyder, Carl, *Capitalism the Creator* (New York, 1940).

Soule, George, *Prosperity Decade . . . 1917-1929* (New York, 1947).

Taylor, George R., *The Transportation Revolution, 1815-1860*. (New York, 1951).

Wright, Chester W., *Economic History of the United States*, new 2nd ed. (New York, 1948).

Wright, David McC., *Capitalism* (New York, 1951).

INDEX

VAN NOSTRAND ANVIL BOOKS already published

1 *MAKING OF MODERN FRENCH MIND*—Kohn
2 *THE AMERICAN REVOLUTION*—Morris
3 *THE LATE VICTORIANS*—Ausubel
4 *WORLD IN THE 20th CENTURY*—Rev. Ed. Snyder
5 *50 DOCUMENTS OF THE 20th CENTURY*—Snyder
6 *THE AGE OF REASON*—Snyder
7 *MARX AND THE MARXISTS*—Hook
8 *NATIONALISM*—Kohn
9 *MODERN JAPAN*—Rev. Ed. Tiedemann
10 *50 DOCUMENTS OF THE 19th CENTURY*—Snyder
11 *CONSERVATISM*—Viereck
12 *THE PAPACY*—Corbett
13 *AGE OF THE REFORMATION*—Bainton
14 *DOCUMENTS IN AMERICAN HISTORY*—Morris
15 *CONTEMPORARY AFRICA*—Rev. Ed. Wallbank
16 *THE RUSSIAN REVOLUTIONS OF 1917*—Curtiss
17 *THE GREEK MIND*—Agard
18 *BRITISH CONSTITUTIONAL HISTORY SINCE 1832*—Schuyler and Weston
19 *THE NEGRO IN THE U.S.*—Logan
20 *AMERICAN CAPITALISM*—Hacker
21 *LIBERALISM*—Schapiro
22 *THE FRENCH REVOLUTION, 1789-1799*—Gershoy
23 *HISTORY OF MODERN GERMANY*—Snyder
24 *HISTORY OF MODERN RUSSIA*—Kohn
25 *NORTH ATLANTIC CIVILIZATION*—Kraus
26 *NATO*—Salvadori
27 *DOCUMENTS IN U.S. FOREIGN POLICY*—Brockway
28 *AMERICAN FARMERS' MOVEMENTS*—Shannon
29 *HISTORIC DECISIONS OF SUPREME COURT*—Swisher
30 *MEDIEVAL TOWN*—Mundy and Riesenberg
31 *REVOLUTION AND REACTION 1848-1852*—Bruun
32 *SOUTHEAST ASIA AND WORLD TODAY*—Buss
33 *HISTORIC DOCUMENTS OF W. W. I*—Snyder
34 *HISTORIC DOCUMENTS OF W. W. II*—Langsam
35 *ROMAN MIND AT WORK*—MacKendrick
36 *SHORT HISTORY OF CANADA*—Masters
37 *WESTWARD MOVEMENT IN U.S.*—Billington
38 *DOCUMENTS IN MEDIEVAL HISTORY*—Downs
39 *HISTORY OF AMERICAN BUSINESS*—Cochran
40 *DOCUMENTS IN CANADIAN HISTORY*—Talman
41 *FOUNDATIONS OF ISRAEL*—Janowsky
42 *MODERN CHINA*—Rowe
43 *BASIC HISTORY OF OLD SOUTH*—Stephenson
44 *THE BENELUX COUNTRIES*—Eyck
45 *MEXICO AND THE CARIBBEAN*—Hanke
46 *SOUTH AMERICA*—Hanke
47 *SOVIET FOREIGN POLICY, 1917-1941*—Kennan
48 *THE ERA OF REFORM, 1830-1860*—Commager
49 *EARLY CHRISTIANITY*—Bainton
50 *RISE AND FALL OF THE ROMANOVS*—Mazour
51 *CARDINAL DOCUMENTS IN BRITISH HISTORY*—Schuyler and Weston
52 *HABSBURG EMPIRE 1804-1918*—Kohn
53 *CAVOUR AND UNIFICATION OF ITALY*—Salvadori
54 *ERA OF CHARLEMAGNE*—Easton and Wieruszowski
55 *MAJOR DOCUMENTS IN AMERICAN ECONOMIC HISTORY, Vol. I*—Hacker
56 *MAJOR DOCUMENTS IN AMERICAN ECONOMIC HISTORY, Vol. II*—Hacker
57 *HISTORY OF THE CONFEDERACY*—Vandiver
58 *COLD WAR DIPLOMACY*—Graebner
59 *MOVEMENTS OF SOCIAL DISSENT IN MODERN EUROPE*—Schapiro
60 *MEDIEVAL COMMERCE*—Adelson
61 *THE PEOPLE'S REPUBLIC OF CHINA*—Buss
62 *WORLD COMMUNISM*—Hook
63 *ISLAM AND THE WEST*—Hitti